The Practitioner Inquiry Series

Marilyn Cochran-Smith and Susan L. Lytle, Series Editors

(continued)

ACTION RESEARCH IN SPECIAL EDUCATION

An Inquiry Approach for Effective Teaching and Learning

Susan M. Bruce
Gerald J. Pine

Teachers College
Columbia University
New York and London

Published by Teachers College Press, 1234 Amsterdam Avenue, New York, NY 10027

Library of Congress Cataloging-in-Publication Data

Bruce, Susan M., 1954–
   Action research in special education : an inquiry approach for effective teaching and learning / Susan M. Bruce and Gerald J. Pine.
       p. cm. — (The practitioner inquiry series)
   Includes bibliographical references and index.
   ISBN 978-0-8077-5091-9 (pbk. : alk. paper) — ISBN 978-0-8077-5092-6 (hardcover : alk. paper) 1. Action research in education. 2. Special education—Research. I. Pine, Gerald J. II. Title.
   LB1028.4.B78 2010
   371.907′2--dc22

                                                                2010013986

ISBN 978-0-8077-5091-9 (paperback)
ISBN 978-0-8077-5092-6 (hardcover)

Printed on acid-free paper

Manufactured in the United States of America

17 16 15 14 13 12 11 10   8 7 6 5 4 3 2 1

This book is dedicated to Gerald J. Pine, Ed.D., who was born on June 1, 1933, and passed on April 11, 2009, during the writing of this book. Jerry was a devoted husband, father, grandfather, and brother. He was also a revered colleague at Boston College and one of the kindest people you could ever meet. Thank you, Jerry, for all you contributed through your teaching, research, service, and friendship.

Contents

Preface

This book is the first of its kind—a book about action research that is specific to the experiences of children with disabilities and the general educators, special educators, and related service professionals who support their learning. While all teachers may benefit from the content of this book, it was written for the special educator. This book emerged out of conversations between two colleagues, one prepared in counseling psychology and general education and the other prepared in general education and special education. This effort was grounded in our mutual commitment to prepare teachers who engage in inquiry.

Action research is an approach to research that does not dictate research design, although some designs are more compatible with the philosophy of action research than others. Action research is a process of concurrently engaging in inquiry about problems and taking actions to solve those problems. It is intentional, sustained, dynamic, and recursive. Action research is about student learning, but it is also about teacher learning. In keeping with our respect for the importance of teacher reflection and learning, our book is sprinkled with quotes from teachers about their experiences as action researchers, and Chapters 5 through 8 are examples of actual teacher-researcher studies.

Chapter 1 provides the reader with a brief history of the evolution of action research outside and inside the field of education, a grounding that is necessary for full appreciation of its philosophical and theoretical roots. This chapter traces the contributions of Bacon, Dewey, Collier, Lewin, Sprague Mitchell, Corey, Schaefer, Stenhouse, Elliott, Cochran-Smith, and Lytle to the development of action research. The chapter concludes with a discussion of the role of case study, a common action research design in special education. Emphasis is placed on the promise of action research to address complex issues faced by children with disabilities and their teachers.

Chapter 2 begins with an introduction to four types of action research: classroom action research, collaborative action research, critical action research, and participatory action research (including studies that are emancipatory). This chapter provides an illustrative discussion of the existing peer-reviewed studies organized within the following four topical themes: (1) assessment and instruction in the content areas, (2) supporting improved behavioral and socialization outcomes, (3) inclusion, and (4) amplifying the voices of children with disabilities. Chapter 2 concludes by examining how the four types of action research can be applied to address one social justice issue, disproportionality.

Chapter 3 provides guidance about how to conduct action research. It is the "how to" chapter of this text, and it is intended to support the classroom action research efforts of either preservice or inservice teachers. The following topics are addressed: identifying the inquiry topic; framing the research question; developing the theoretical framework; developing the action research plan (including selection of data sources and ethical conduct of research); collecting, organizing, and analyzing data; drawing conclusions and meaning making; sharing findings; and evaluating the action research study.

Chapter 4 discusses the connections among reflection, inquiry, and action research within the teacher preparation program in special education. By participating in the conceptualization and implementation of action research, teacher candidates construct their roles, including how they will approach dilemmas in the classroom. Experiences from two teacher education programs are shared in the second half of this chapter. The programs' efforts in action research are illustrated by sharing content on school mission and department themes (and their connection to inquiry and action research), processes (such as faculty responsibilities for the inquiry component), and grading procedures. A sample grading rubric is shared.

Chapters 5 through 8 are sample action research studies that were conducted by master's degree students at Boston College. Three of these studies were written by students majoring in special education and one was written by a general education major with classroom experience in special education. These studies focus on children with mild to severe disabilities across curricular areas and grade levels. A more detailed introduction to each of these studies precedes Chapter 5.

The afterword begins with a discussion of some of the unique characteristics of conducting action research about and with children and young adults with disabilities. The chapter concludes with suggestions for future research, based on the literature reviewed in Chapter 2 and organized with the themes of (1) assessment and instruction in the content areas, (2) supporting improved behavioral and socialization outcomes, (3) inclusion, (4) amplifying the voices of children with disabilities, and (5) additional social justice issues.

Acknowledgments

We would like to first acknowledge the cooperating teachers, field supervisors, instructors of the inquiry courses, and the Department of Teacher Education, Special Education, Curriculum & Instruction faculty at Boston College for their contributions to the inquiry courses. Special recognition goes to the following individuals who were instrumental in supporting the inquiry of the four graduate student authors whose work is featured in this book: Marty Laughrey, Eileen Stokes, Don Ricciato, Tina Fiscella, Hilary Shea, Carolyn Russo, Rachel Carpenter, and Claudia Rinaldi. We would also like to thank Audrey Friedman, Patrick McQuillan, Sarah Enterline, and Maria Estella Brisk for their thoughtful input to the revision of the inquiry courses. We would like to acknowledge our department colleagues for their ongoing devotion to preparing teachers who are reflective practitioners with a deep commitment to addressing issues of social justice.

We also want to recognize the contributions of the Teachers for a New Era project, led by Marilyn Cochran-Smith with data analysis supports from Larry Ludlow and others from the Department of Educational Research and Measurement at Boston College. Data on the inquiry experiences of our students have been instrumental to revising the courses and to our larger efforts in embedding inquiry experiences across coursework. We also thank the many doctoral students across departments who contributed to the data collection and data analysis for that project. Special recognition goes to Joan Barnett and Sarah Enterline, who devoted great energy to the project and who supported faculty in discussing the implications of findings.

We are also very grateful to Cynthia Pearl, the University of Central Florida, and the Bureau of Exceptional Education of the Florida Department of Education for sharing their expertise in preparing reflective practitioners.

A special note of appreciation goes to Brian Ellerbeck, Executive Acquisitions Editor, Teachers College Press, for his detailed feedback and

support of this project. We are also thankful to the many other professionals at Teachers College Press who have worked on the editing and
indexing of this book.

We would also like to thank our family members for their emotional
support. A special note of thanks goes to Jerry's wife, Mary Pine, and to
my mother, Dorothy Firth, whose kind words were so very encouraging.

PART I

INQUIRY AND ACTION RESEARCH IN SPECIAL EDUCATION

Action research has a rich history, grounded in concerns about important social justice issues. Part I of this book provides the reader with historical and theoretical grounding and practical information about conducting action research in special education. Chapter 1 traces the development of educational action research from its social justice roots. Chapter 2 suggests a schema for action research in special education. This is followed by an illustrative review of action research studies in special education, organized by four themes: assessment and instruction in the content areas; improved behavioral and socialization outcomes; inclusion; and amplifying the voices of children with disabilities. Chapter 2 concludes with a description about how different types of action research in special education could be applied to address one social justice issue in special education, disproportionality. Chapter 3 is a "how to" chapter, walking the reader through the process of conducting action research, with an emphasis on classroom action research. Chapter 4 shares how preparation in action research fits within a larger emphasis on preparing reflective teachers who engage in inquiry. This chapter concludes with a description of the action research component of two university teacher preparation programs.

1

Action Research: Promise for Special Education

Gerald J. Pine

Action research and special education are animated by a deep and abiding ethos of social justice. Within the context and practice of special education, action research can make a meaningful difference in the lives of teachers and their students with special needs. Conducting action research to address special education teaching and learning issues reflects the ideals and values of Francis Bacon, who in the 17th century asserted that knowledge and inquiry must be motivated by charity—human knowledge should be in service of or love for one's fellow human beings. For Bacon the purposes of human inquiry and knowledge are to reduce human suffering, increase the quality of human life, enhance the well-being of humans, and advance human capacities (Bell, 1991).

What is action research? Action research is a process of concurrently inquiring about problems and taking action to solve them. It is an intentional, sustained, recursive, and dynamic process of inquiry in which the teacher takes an action—purposefully and ethically in a specific classroom context—to improve teaching/learning (Mills, 2003). Figure 1.1 is Hingley's (2008) modification of the action research cycle originally depicted by Carr and Kemmis (1986, p. 186). Action research is change research, a nonlinear recursive cyclical process of study designed to achieve concrete change in a specific situation, context, or work setting to improve teaching/learning. It seeks to improve practice, the understanding of practice by its practitioners, and the situations in which practice is located (Carr & Kemmis, 1986; Cole & Knowles, 2000).

While focused on actions leading to change, action research is also a mental disposition—a way of being in the classroom and the school, a lifelong habit of inquiry. It is recursive in that teacher researchers frequently work simultaneously within several research steps and circle back to readdress issues and modify research questions based on reflection for, reflection in, and reflection on action. The reflection–action–reflection–action process can be considered a spiraling cyclical process in which research issues change and actions are improved, discarded, or

Figure 1.1. Action Research Cycles

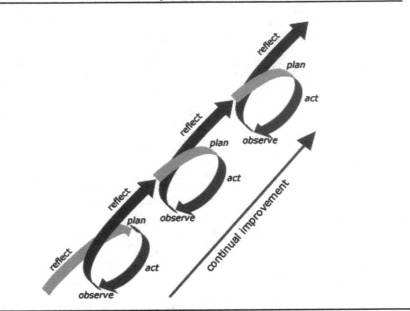

become more focused. In education, action research generates action-able hypotheses about teaching, learning, and curriculum from reflection on and study of teaching, learning, and curriculum to improve teaching, learning, and curriculum.

Action research challenges certain assumptions about the research process and educational change (Grundy, 1994). It challenges the separation of research from action, the separation of the researcher from the researched, assumptions about control of knowledge, and assumptions about the nature of educational reform. "Action research is by, with, of and for people, rather than on people" (Reason & Bradbury, 2001, p. 2).

Action research assumes that teachers are the agents and source of educational reform and not the objects of reform. Action research empowers teachers to own professional knowledge because teachers through the process of action inquiry conceptualize and create knowledge, interact around knowledge, transform knowledge, and apply knowledge. Action research enables teachers to reflect on their practice to improve it, become more autonomous in professional judgment, develop a more energetic and dynamic environment for teaching and learning, articulate and build their craft knowledge, and recognize and appreciate their own expertise. Inquiry through action research is a powerful context for ongoing teacher development (Cole & Knowles, 2000). "Action Research enacts systematic inquiry in ways that are democratic, participatory, empowering, and life enhancing" (Stringer, 2004, p. 31). It assumes that practice is embedded in the science of the unique, recognizing that human events are idiosyncratic—they vary with time, place, cultural circumstances, the ecology of the moment, serendipity, obliquities, and unforeseen circumstances.

Action research is well suited to the complex, personal, contextual, and moral aspects of teaching (Cole & Knowles, 2000). Action research assumes that caring knowledge is contextual knowledge, with the understanding that human actions always take place in context and must be understood in context. It assumes that knowledge is tentative and probabilistic, and continually subject to modification. It views "not knowing" and ambiguity as resources for learning. Action research assumes that teacher development involves lifelong learning in changing and multidimensional contexts. It is grounded in the reality of the school, classroom, teachers, and students. It is a process in which study and inquiry lead to actions that make a difference in teaching and learning and bridge doing (practice), learning (study), and reflection (inquiry). Action research reflects deliberate attention to the ways in which what we know is caught up in what we do and who we are. Through action research we intellectually and affectively nurture our students, our classrooms, and ourselves. Classrooms and schools become sites where new meanings and understandings are created and shared.

In educational action research, teachers, who traditionally have been the subjects of research, conduct research on their own situations and circumstances in their classrooms and schools. They conduct their research according to Lewin's basic dictum, "No research without action—no action without research" (as cited in Marrow, 1969, p. 10). Teachers are privileged through the action research process to produce knowledge and consequently experience that "knowledge is power." As knowledge and action are joined in changing practice, there is growing recognition of the power of teachers to change and reform education from the inside rather than having change and reform imposed top down from the outside. Through action research, "teachers transcend the truth of power through the power of truth" (Whitehead, 1993, p. 86).

THE SOCIAL JUSTICE ROOTS OF ACTION RESEARCH

Action research is rooted in a concern for social justice. Indeed, social justice historically permeated action research. This action-oriented form of inquiry originated outside the field of education in the work of John Collier, social worker, anthropologist, and author. After holding several positions in community organizations, serving as the executive secretary of the American Indian Defense Association, and editing the magazine *American Indian Life*, Collier was appointed in 1933 by Franklin D. Roosevelt as the United States Commissioner for Indian Affairs, a position he held for 12 years, making him the longest-serving commissioner. Reversing federal Indian policies, his "Indian New Deal" approach officially rescinded the repression of American Indian language and promoted tribal self-government, cultural preservation, and religious freedom for Native Americans.

Appalled by the egregious record of the U.S. government's inhumane treatment of the American Indian, Collier (1945) developed a collaborative action research approach designed to reverse deeply discriminatory, racist, and destructive practices and to restore the integrity and dignity of Indian society and culture. In his efforts to establish a living democracy in Indian societies and to implement more democratic policies and approaches in the Bureau of Indian Affairs, he saw action research as an imperative.

> We had in mind a particular kind of research, or, if you will, particular conditions. We had in mind research impelled from central areas of needed action. And since action is by nature not only specialized but also integrative of specialties, and nearly always integrative of more than specialties, our needed research must be of the integrative sort. Again, since the findings of the research must be carried into effect by the administrators and the layman, and must be criticized by them through their experience, the administrator and the layman must themselves participate creatively in the research, impelled as it is from their own area of need . . . such research has invariably operated to deepen our realization of the potentialities of the democratic way, as well as our realization of our own extreme, pathetic shortcomings. (Collier, 1945, pp. 275–276)

Collier's collaborative model of inquiry was a congenial match with the goals of social psychologist Kurt Lewin, who studied the dynamics of group interaction seeking to counteract racism. Lewin was familiar with Collier's work in action research, referring to it approvingly in an article he wrote on action research, and minority problems (Lewin, 1946). Both Collier and Lewin shared the conviction that action research could strengthen democratic relationships. During the 1930s and 1940s, Lewin and his colleagues developed the concept of action research as a way to study and improve group and intergroup relations and to address conflict, crises, and change. They viewed action research as a collaborative process in which participants could work together to understand and solve social and organizational problems by conducting studies of their own situations and circumstances.

In 1944, Lewin established a Research Center for Group Dynamics at the Massachusetts Institute of Technology (MIT), where he and his staff launched action research projects to combat racial discrimination and to improve intergroup relationships (Lewin, 1945). These studies focused on such issues as anti-Semitic gang behavior, resistance to hiring black sales personnel, the effects of integrated versus segregated public housing, the socialization of street gangs, the cause and cure of prejudice in children, and ways of dealing with public remarks made by bigots.

> Lewin was particularly concerned to raise the self-esteem of minority groups, to help them seek "independence, equality and co-operation" through action research and other means. He wanted minority groups to overcome the forces of "exploitation" and colonization that had been prominent in their modern histories. (Adelman, 1993, pp. 7–8)

Research, for Lewin, was learning by doing for the purpose of addressing and resolving important social issues (Noffke, 1997).

Lewin (1946) introduced and coined the term "action research" in his article on action research and minority problems, in which he described the action research process as a spiral of steps, including planning, action, and fact-finding about the result of the action. He articulated a process that involved a spiral of steps or cycles that consisted of identifying a general idea, reconnaissance, general planning, developing the first action step, implementing the first action step, evaluation, and revising the general plan. From this basic cycle the researchers then spiral into a second cycle of activities: developing the second action step, implementing, evaluating, revising the general plan, developing the third action step, implementing, evaluating, and so on, continuing into a third, fourth, or fifth cycle of activities. Lewin's work affirmed the idea that a practitioner's reflection on knowing and reflection in action can lead to actionable theory that can be generalized to other situations (Noffke, 1997).

THE DEVELOPMENT OF
ACTION RESEARCH IN EDUCATION

Perhaps the earliest effort to engage teachers as researchers can be found in the work of Lucy Sprague Mitchell. She had been the first Dean of Women at the University of California, Berkeley and was friendly with John Dewey and greatly influenced by his writings. Committing her life to improving schools for children, she established the Bureau of Educational Experiments in New York City in 1916. She gathered a team of psychologists, a social worker, a doctor, and a number of classroom teachers around her to study jointly, in as free an atmosphere as possible, children, children's language development, teaching, and a variety of new experimental approaches to education. Eventually, over time, while continuing to conduct research, the bureau's mission expanded to developing a model teacher education program that ultimately became the foundation for the establishment of the Bank Street College of Education.

Building on the work of Collier and Lewin, Corey and others at Teachers College, Columbia University, developed collaborative action research studies that brought together teachers and professors to improve curriculum, instruction, and field supervision (Corey, 1953). Corey advanced action research as an alternative to traditional research in schools, based on the belief that "research methodology will not begin to have the influence it might have on American education until thousands of teachers, administrators, and supervisors make more frequent use of the method of science in solving their own practical problems" (Corey, p. 18). Recognizing teachers' reluctance to implement someone else's ideas in their classrooms, Corey vigorously argued that teachers should be equal partners in cooperative action research, including participation in the design of classroom research and in data collection and interpretation.

Corey (1953) viewed action research as a recursive process proceeding through spiraling cycles of planning, actions, reflections, and change, reflected in the following five stages:

- Identifying a problem area about which an individual or a group would be sufficiently concerned to want to take action.
- Selecting a specific problem, formulating a hypothesis, and specifying a goal and a procedure for reaching it.
- Carefully recording the actions taken and gathering and analyzing data to determine the degree to which the goal has been achieved.
- Inferring from the evidence collected generalizations regarding the relationship between the actions and the desired goal.
- Continually retesting these generalizations in action situations. (pp. 40–41)

Within the stages articulated by Corey, problems, hypotheses, questions, and actions could be changed, reflecting the recursive nature of the research, with each cycle of research affecting previous and subsequent cycles. Similar to Lewin's conception of spiraling cycles, the stages are not linear but rather are considered as interacting loops of research activities.

In his book *The School as a Center of Inquiry*, Schaefer (1967) extended the concept of action research to make it an integral part of the school culture, suggesting that teachers use action research to make schools collegial centers of inquiry. He argued:

> We can no longer afford to conceive of the schools simply as distribution centers for dispensing cultural orientation, information, and knowledge developed by other units. The complexities of teaching and learning in formal classrooms have become so formidable and the intellectual demands upon the system so enormous that the school must be much more than a place of instruction. It must be a center of inquiry—a producer as well as a transmitter of knowledge. (p. 1)

Schaefer urged that students as well as teachers become involved in academic inquiry and that experimentation with learning and teaching become the school norm. Through inquiry, collaborating teachers would design new instructional approaches and curriculum materials and try them out to see what worked and what didn't work. Their work would then inform further inquiry and trials, and their schools would become "knowledge creating schools" in which the intellectual assets of teachers would be deeply valued and supported (Hargreaves, 2001).

Embedded in action research is Dewey's idea of inquiry—thought intertwined with action, reflection in and on action—which proceeds from doubt to the resolution of doubt, to the generation of new doubt. Inquiry begins with situations that are problematic, that are confusing, uncertain, conflicted, and block the free flow of action.

> The inquirer is in, and in transaction with, the problematic situation. He or she must construct the meaning and frame the problem of the situation, thereby setting the stage for problem solving, which in combination with changes in the external context, brings a new problematic situation into being. Hence the proper test of a round of inquiry is not only "Have I solved this problem?" but "Do I like the new problems I've created?" (Schon, 1995, p. 31)

Hence the notion of action research as a habit of continuing inquiry—a Deweyan attitude of questioning one's practice that teacher researcher Carol Battaglia (1995) embraces:

> I now believe that action research is as much a process of asking questions about one's practice, as it is deciding what to do about solutions. Action research enables you to live your questions; in a way they become the focal point of your thinking. My questions took on an almost mantra-like quality; they seemed to seep into my thinking and conversation, creep into my reading and writing when I'd least expect it They also kept me focused. I appre-

ciate how professionally healthy it might be to adopt an "action research mentality" whereby one is always thinking or attempting to polish another facet of the work one does. Perhaps then action research is an attitude or becomes an attitude that is brought to one's practice. (p. 107)

CONTEMPORARY TEACHER RESEARCH

The contemporary teacher-as-researcher movement began in England with the work of Stenhouse (1971, 1975) and the Humanities Curriculum Project. Stenhouse, who coined the term "teacher-as-researcher," believed that teaching should be based on research, that the classroom was a natural laboratory for the study of teaching and learning, and that research and curriculum development were the privileged preserve of teachers (Stenhouse, 1988). Building on the work of Stenhouse, the Ford Teaching Project evolved to focus on the self-monitoring role of teachers who examined their practices in collaborative action research study groups (Elliott, 2006; Elliott & Adelman, 1975). The work of Stenhouse and Elliott migrated to the United States, where it stimulated the further development and refinement of the concept of the teacher-as-researcher.

As a burgeoning movement in the United States, teacher research has been defined by Cochran-Smith and Lytle (1993) as "systematic intentional inquiry by teachers about their own school and classroom work" (pp. 23–24). It is systematic in that it involves ordered ways of gathering data, documenting experiences, and producing a written record. It is intentional in that the research is planned and deliberate rather than spontaneous. It is inquiry in that the research emanates from or generates questions and "reflects teachers' desires to make sense of their experiences—to adopt a learning stance of openness toward classroom life" (Cochran-Smith & Lytle, 1993, p. 24)

Cochran-Smith and Lytle offer a working typology of teacher research that groups four types of teacher research into two broad categories: conceptual and empirical research. *Conceptual research* refers to theoretical/philosophical work or the analysis of ideas. *Empirical research* refers to the collection, analysis, and interpretation of data gathered from teachers' own classrooms and schools. Empirical research includes journals, oral inquiries, and classroom/school studies. Journals are teachers' written accounts of classroom life over time, including records of observation, analyses of experiences, and reflections and interpretations of practices. Oral inquiries are teachers' oral examinations of classroom/social issues, contexts, texts, and experiences, including collaborative analyses and interpretations and explorations between cases and theories. Classroom/ school studies are teachers' explorations of practice-based issues using data based on observation, interview, and document collection involving individual or collaborative work. The focus of conceptual research is essays that deal with teachers' interpretations of the assumptions and characteristics of classroom and school life and/or the research itself.

Cochran-Smith and Lytle (1993) place great emphasis on teachers' ways of knowing, teacher knowing through systematic subjectivity, and teacher *emic*, or "insider's perspective that makes visible the ways students and teachers together construct knowledge and curriculum" (p. 43). They distinguish among three conceptions of teacher learning. The first of these is *knowledge for practice*, in which university researchers generate formal knowledge and theory for teachers to use in order to improve practice. Within this conception of teacher learning, teachers are viewed primarily as consumers of research.

The second conception is *knowledge in practice*, in which the emphasis is on knowledge in action—knowledge that is embedded in the exemplary practice of experienced teachers. The knowledge in action concept suggests that good teaching can be coached and learned through reflective supervision or through a process of coaching reflective teaching. Learning is viewed as assisted performance. Both of these conceptions of teacher learning are hierarchical, distinguishing between expert and novice teachers as well as formal and practical knowledge.

The third conception of teacher learning is *knowledge of practice*, which assumes "that the knowledge teachers need to teach well emanates from systematic inquiries about teaching, learners and learning, subject matter and curriculum, and schools and schooling. This knowledge is constructed collectively within local and broader communities" (Cochran-Smith & Lytle, 1999, p. 279). Within this conception of teacher learning there are no distinctions between formal and practical knowledge. Teachers are viewed as constructors and generators of knowledge and curriculum. Knowledge of practice and teacher research are viewed as mutually interchangeable. Cochran-Smith and Lytle (1999) argue that teacher inquiry is a powerful way of articulating local knowledge and for redefining and creating a new knowledge base for teaching and learning.

One of the most distinctive and significant contributions Cochran-Smith and Lytle (1999) make to the teacher-as-researcher movement is their construct of *inquiry as stance*. Inquiry as stance suggests an orientation to the construction of knowledge and its relationship to practice. With this stance the work of teachers in generating local knowledge through inquiry communities is considered social and political, "making problematic the current arrangements of schooling, the ways knowledge is constructed, evaluated, and used, and teachers' individual and collective roles in bringing about change" (Cochran-Smith, 2002, p. 15). Inquiry as stance positions teachers to link their inquiry to larger questions about the ends of teacher learning in school reform and to larger social, political, and intellectual movements, emphasizing that teacher learning for the next century needs to be understood as a long-term collective project with a democratic agenda (Cochran-Smith & Lytle, 2009).

The outcomes emerging from an inquiry stance are transformative (Cochran-Smith, 2002). One outcome is that teachers learn to raise questions and try to change routine practices, challenging common expectations and reconceptualizing what teaching and learning are all about. A second outcome is that teachers question and challenge the external assumptions, values, and beliefs held by others regarding practice and the internal assumptions, values, and beliefs held by teachers themselves. Finally, an inquiry stance raises teachers' consciousness and develops awareness that decisions regarding all dimensions of teaching and learning need to weigh complex and conflicting values, information, and viewpoints. The inquiry stance characterizing teacher-as-researcher is more than an attitude and posture regarding inquiry; it is a transformative worldview of knowledge construction, teaching practice, and the nature of learning.

ACTION RESEARCH, SPECIAL EDUCATION, AND THE CASE STUDY

Special education research is a difficult-to-do science. There is great variability in participants due to ability and disability characteristics and racial, ethnic, and linguistic diversity. How, then, does action research address the complexity of special education? One prominent action research approach to address individual variability and complexity in special education is the case study. Within the context of special education, almost by definition, teacher action research is case study research with the individual child as the unit of analysis. In addressing the needs of children with disabilities, the case study is a powerful research methodology for sparking interplay between thought and action, helping to develop increased capacities of analysis, which make educational change actions possible (Abramson, 1992; Merriam, 1998; Stake, 1995). The case study is an empirical approach to studying contemporary phenomena within real-life contexts (Yin, 1984). But the case study is more than an empirical approach. "Case study is the way of the artist, who achieves greatness when, through the portrayal of a single instance locked in time and circumstance, he communicates enduring truths about the human condition. For both scientist and artist, content and intent emerge in form" (McDonald & Walker, 1975, p. 3).

The history of the social sciences is filled with dramatic "artistic" conceptual "breakthroughs" that have emanated from the use of the case study. The intellectual contributions of Freud, Piaget, Maslow, Erickson, Jung, Adler, and Rogers are examples of profound influential thinking and seminal ideas that were born and nurtured through the case study approach. When we look at other professions we find, for example, that the research literature of law is the deliberate elaborate explanation of cases, that the research literature of medicine is the deliberate explanation of cases, and that case study research is the predominant teaching resource in MBA programs across the country. The case study is a congenial approach for the person of action, for the person who engages life, who tries out ideas, reflects on their implementation, and tries again. The cycle of thought-action-thought finds comfortable embrace in the case study, a basic methodology for action research.

The greatest use of the case study by the teacher researcher would be in the study of the individual. In a profession where there is a basic commitment to teaching and understanding individual students and situations, it is case study research devoted to the full study of individuals that offers a comfortable and rewarding action research approach for teacher researchers. The full study of individual students enables teachers to function as clinical researchers in examining the wide range of contextual and multidimensional variables that impinge on student learning and development. The case study provides a sound action research base for generating new hypotheses about student learning and growth.

The careful and caring attention given to the individual learner through the case study approach cultivates habits of mind that carry over to a way of regarding other children; a changed attitude about children as learners and people; a way of working with children that is deeper, more connected to the child, and more respectful and honoring of the individual child; and a way that makes us more humble about what we think we know about children.

REFERENCES

Abramson, P. R. (1992). *A case for case studies.* Thousand Oaks, CA: Sage.

Adelman, C. (1993). Kurt Lewin and the origins of action research. *Educational Action Research, 1*(1), 7–24.

Battaglia, C. (1995). Confused on a higher level about more important things. In S. E. Noffke & R. B. Stevenson (Eds.), *Educational action research: Becoming practically critical* (pp. 74–93). New York: Teachers College Press.

Bell, D. (1991). *The winding passage: Sociological essays and journeys.* New Brunswick, NJ: Transaction.

Carr, W., & Kemmis, S. (1986). *Becoming critical: Education knowledge and action research*. Philadelphia: Falmer Press.

Cochran-Smith, M. (2002). Inquiry and outcomes: Learning to teach in the age of accountability. *Teacher Education and Practice, 15*(4), 12–34.

Cochran-Smith, M., & Lytle, S. L. (1993). *Inside/outside: Teacher research and knowledge*. New York: Teachers College Press.

Cochran-Smith, M., & Lytle, S. L. (1999). Relationships of knowledge and practice: Teacher learning in communities. *Review of Research, 24,* 249–305.

Cochran-Smith, M., & Lytle, S. L. (2009). *Inquiry as stance: Practitioner research for the next generation*. New York: Teachers College Press.

Cole, A. L., & Knowles, J. G. (2000). *Researching teaching: Exploring teacher development through reflexive inquiry*. Boston: Allyn and Bacon.

Collier, J. (1945). United States Indian Administration as a laboratory of ethnic relations. *Social Research, 12*(3), 265–303.

Corey, S. (1953). *Action research to improve school practices*. New York: Teachers College Press.

Elliott, J. (2006). *Reflecting where the action is: The selected works of John Elliott*. New York: Routledge.

Elliott, J., & Adelman, C. (1975). *Classroom action research. Cambridge: Ford Teaching Project*, Cambridge, UK: Cambridge Institute of Education.

Grundy, S. (1994). Action research at the school level: Possibilities and problems. *Educational Action Research, 2*(1), 23–38.

Hargreaves, D. H. (2001). A capital theory of school effectiveness and improvement. *British Educational Research Journal, 27*(4), 487–503.

Hingley, V. (2008). Action research diagrams. Retrieved June 2, 2009, from The Higher Education Academy: Leisure, Sport and Tourism Network Web site: http://heacademy.ac.uk/assets/hlst/documents/heinfe_exchange/act_res_cycle.doc

Lewin, K. (1945). The research center for group dynamics at Massachusetts Institute of Technology. *Sociometry, 2,* 126–136.

Lewin, K. (1946). Action research and minority problems. *Journal of Social Issues, 2,* 34–46.

Marrow, A. J. (1969). *The practical theorist: The life and work of Kurt Lewin*. New York: Basic Books.

McDonald, B., & Walker, R. (1975). Case study and the social philosophy of educational research. *Cambridge Journal of Education, 5,*(1), 2–11.

Merriam, S. B. (1998). *Qualitative research and case study applications in education*. San Francisco: Jossey-Bass.

Mills, G. E. (2003). *Action research: A guide for the teacher researcher* (2nd ed.). Upper Saddle River, NJ: Prentice Hall.

Noffke, S. E. (1997). Themes and tensions in U.S. action research: Towards historical analysis. In S. Hollingsworth (Ed.), *International action research: a casebook for educational reform*. London: Falmer Press.

Reason, P. & Bradbury, H. (Eds.) (2001). *Handbook of action research: Concise paperback edition*. Thousand Oaks, CA: Sage.

Schaefer, R. L. (1967). *The school as a center of inquiry*. New York: Harper & Row.

Schon, D. A. (1995). The new scholarship requires a new epistemology. *Change, 27*(6), 29–34.

Stake, R. E. (1995). *The art of case study research.* Thousand Oaks, CA: Sage.

Stenhouse, L. (1971). The Humanities Curriculum Project: The rationale. *Theory into Practice, 10*(3), 154–162.

Stenhouse, L. (1975). *An introduction to curriculum research and development.* London: Heinemann.

Stenhouse, L. (1988). Artistry and teaching: The teacher as focus of research and development. *Journal of Curriculum and Supervision, 4*(1), 43–51.

Stringer, E. (2004). *Action research in education.* Upper Saddle River, NJ: Pearson Education.

Whitehead, J. (1993). *The growth of educational knowledge.* Bournemouth, Dorset, UK: Hyde Publications.

Yin, R. K. (1984). *Case study research: Design and methods.* Thousand Oaks, CA: Sage.

2

Improving Opportunities for Children with Disabilities Through Action Research

Susan M. Bruce

Action research is a powerful approach for addressing critical issues experienced by children with disabilities. The recursive nature of action research makes it an ideal approach to use when seeking solutions to complex problems that occur in complex contexts such as classrooms. The recursive quality creates opportunities for teachers to change their instructional focus or approach in response to new understandings that emerge from multiple cycles of reflection and action. Thus, action research supports teachers and other educational professionals to make meaningful changes in practice in response to data on student learning. In addition to addressing learning outcomes in the classroom, action research is well suited to address more systemic social justice issues. This chapter begins by presenting an action research schema that is useful to thinking about action research in special education. A discussion of the existing action research studies about children with disabilities follows, organized within four topical themes, with connections made to the types of action research presented in the schema. This chapter concludes with a discussion about how each type of action research can be applied to address the problem of disproportionality, a social justice issue of importance to general and special educators, parents, and children at risk for identification of a disability.

A SCHEMA FOR ACTION RESEARCH IN SPECIAL EDUCATION

Various schemas can be used to categorize educational action research. Hendricks's (2009) schema is used here, although the definitions of the categories are broadened to capture the characteristics of action research in special education. Such studies can be categorized as being (1) classroom action research, (2) collaborative action research, (3) critical action research, or (4) participatory action research (Hendricks, 2009).

Classroom action research, also known as *teacher research,* takes place at the classroom level and is conducted by the teacher for the purpose of improving instruction and, subsequently, learning outcomes for children (Hendricks, 2009). Such research may or may not include collaboration with university researchers. Wansart (1995) asserts that classroom action research in special education must move beyond a deficit-driven approach to research that discovers and builds upon the abilities and achievements of children. Teachers discover students' abilities through systematic observation coupled with caring attention to students' stories. This focus on ability is a form of social action that has the power to transform how teachers view students and, more importantly, how students view themselves. Classroom action research in special education must be about student abilities, advocacy, and meaningful changes in how we teach (Wansart, 1995).

Collaborative action research occurs when research with a focus on action is done in partnership with others such as teacher colleagues, parents, related service professionals, or administrators (Hendricks, 2009). Sometimes this type of research involves someone from outside the school, such as a university professor, who joins the research team and brings specialized content knowledge or research expertise to support the effort. Collaborative action research can break up the isolation of teaching by providing educators with an opportunity to engage in critical conversations about practice (Hobson, 2001). "Collaborative action research liberates teachers' creative potential, stimulates their abilities to investigate their own situations, and mobilizes human resources to solve educational problems" (Pine, 2009, p. 128). Based on their own collaborative action research experience, Stevens, Slaton, and Bunney (1992) suggest that organization (of time and materials), clear delineation of roles and responsibilities, frequent communication (including discussions leading to data-based decisions), voluntary participation, and a realistic timeline support the success of collaborative action research studies.

The defining feature of *critical action research* is its emphasis on disparity (Hendricks, 2009) experienced because of prejudice and discrimination based on gender, ethnicity, social class, or disability. Critical action research examines social, political, organizational, and linguistic dimensions that create or sustain inequities (Kemmis & McTaggart, 2005). The goal of critical action research is to cause positive social change. Critical action research can improve opportunities for individuals who are oppressed, including children with disabilities. While collaboration is also essential to critical action research, this collaboration extends beyond the school district or adult agency and the university to involve additional community members who contribute authentic knowledge of the issue and context because of their lived experiences. Parents and siblings of children with disabilities and adults with disabilities may be important participants in critical action research studies in special education.

Participatory action research involves participants (in this case, children or young adults with disabilities) for the purposes of identifying and addressing a problem of concern to them (Hendricks, 2009). Self-determination and advocacy are central tenets of participatory action research (Bruyere, 1993; Porter & Lacey, 2005). Balcazar, Keys, Kaplan, and Suarez-Balcazar (1998) cite the following four foundational principles of participatory action research: (1) individuals with disabilities identify the issues to be studied, (2) individuals with disabilities are directly involved in the research, (3) participation in action research supports individuals with disabilities to identify their relative strengths and resources, which can then be applied to solve the identified problem, and (4) a goal of improving the quality of life for individuals with disabilities. The child's or young adult's level of involvement may vary according to the research design, their knowledge about the research process, and the severity of the participant's disability. Participatory action research challenges special educators to consider issues of student empowerment and an associated shift in educator roles to support students with disabilities to participate in the research process (Park, Meyer, & Goetz, 1998). Because constituents participate in defining the problem to be studied and help to identify potential solutions, participatory action research should result in greater social validity and a narrowing of the gap between research and practice (Balcazar et al., 1998; & Bruyere, 1993). Based on their experience as action researchers, Ward and Trigler (2001) suggest the following strategies as being important to the quality of participatory action research studies: orienting and teaching stakeholders (with disabilities) about the research process, clarifying roles, and negotiating time commitments at the beginning of the research process.

Some distinguish between action research that is participatory and action research that is truly emancipatory (Gilbert, 2004). Emancipatory action research is founded on the social model of disability that asserts that disability is a socially defined construct as opposed to disability being defined by an individual's characteristics. By extension, research that is driven by the social model of disability is controlled by people who have disabilities, with the goal of social change including the emancipation of individuals with disabilities. This necessitates a shift in power between co-researchers (those with and without disabilities) and a direct relationship between individuals with disabilities and funding institutions (Gilbert, 2004; Walmsley, 2001), making emancipatory research generally more appropriate for emancipated adults with disabilities. Barnes (2002) outlines these six guiding principles of disability emancipatory research: (1) accountability to the disability community; (2) adoption of the social model of disability, which examines the social and political contexts that create disability as opposed to viewing disability as being solely within the person; (3) the belief that objectivity requires us to achieve rigor in research while respecting personal experience; (4) implementation of research methods that capture the complexities of daily experiences, including contextual factors that mediate and manipulate the daily experiences of individuals with disabilities; (5) recognition that how one individual experiences disability is influenced by the larger collective experience of all persons with disabilities; and (6) commitment that emancipatory research should produce outcomes that are meaningful for individuals with disabilities. Some of these principles are applicable to critical and participatory action research with a focus on children. Whether one views emancipatory research as a subtype of participatory research or a separate type of action research, there are differences in the degree of control claimed by individuals with disabilities and in the feasibility of research designs. However, both approaches are concerned with advocacy, reciprocity, and issues of power between participants/co-researchers with disabilities and researchers/co-researchers without disabilities (Sample, 1996).

ACTION RESEARCH STUDIES IN SPECIAL EDUCATION

Through reading and reflection on the existing peer-reviewed publications about action research studies in special education, four topical themes emerged. These themes are used here to organize an illustrative rather than exhaustive discussion of the existing action research literature on children with disabilities.

Theme 1: Assessment and Instruction in the Content Areas

Several researchers explored different types of assessments to learn more about how each contributed to understanding student learning. For example, studies by Richter (1997) and Capobianco, Lincoln, Canuel-Browne, and Trimarchi (2006) examined the relative merits of formative and summative assessment while learning about students' affective responses to each type of assessment.

Classroom and collaborative action research studies were applied to improve instruction and student learning outcomes in the content areas. Most of these studies (across the grade levels) addressed literacy. One exception was a mathematics study by Brookhart, Andolina, Zuza, and

Furman (2004), who examined the impact of student self-assessment procedures on memorization of multiplication facts. They discovered that although students' self-assessment improved over time, direct instruction of effective self-assessment was necessary.

Literacy outcomes were addressed through classroom and collaborative action research studies. Literacy studies included the application of technologies (Mortensen, 2002), metacognitive strategies (Welch & Chisholm, 1994), and adult learning about the first language of an English Language Learner (Schoen & Schoen, 2003) to improve writing instruction and student performance. Falk-Ross (2000) improved the oral responses of one student by first teaching adults to provide appropriate cues. The studies by Schoen and Schoen and Falk-Ross featured strong teacher learning components. In these studies, teachers needed time to learn from colleagues and from the literature as preparation to improve instruction for children with disabilities. Several studies trained reading tutors in an effort to increase instructional time invested in reading and to target the needs of individual students (Marchand-Martella, Martella, Orlob, & Ebey; 2000; Osborn, Freeman, Burley, Wilson, Jones, & Rychener, 2007). Moni, Jobling, and van Kraayenoord (2007) and Morgan and Moni (2008) addressed the lack of motivating reading material for adolescents with intellectual disability by developing and implementing individualized and co-constructed personalized text. One participant from the Morgan and Moni study expressed his excitement about personalized text in the following passage:

> Oh, this is so cool. I can't believe I am in a story about motorbikes and that it's about me on an adventure and I'm a dirt bike demon. This is way cool. I'm not doing anything else but read this, and when I finish, I'm taking it home and I'm going to read it again. Let's do it! (p. 97)

Theme 2: Supporting Improved Behavioral and Socialization Outcomes

Behavior and socialization problems are often a reason for exclusion in the school and larger community (Horner & Carr, 1997), making this an important social justice issue. The positive behavior support plans often used to address behavioral and socialization needs are essentially action plans, making this area of concern a natural match for action research designs. While behavior and socialization are frequently a focus of teacher candidates, few peer-reviewed publications on action research studies in this area have been produced. Schoen and Nolen (2004) and Schoen and

Thomas (2006) developed instructional action plans that integrated practices founded in behavioral theory, social learning theory, cognitive learning theory, and humanistic learning theory, combined with consideration of student interests and preferences to improve behavioral outcomes. Cheney (1998) conducted a collaborative action research study with middle school children and their parents to improve behavioral and socialization outcomes. It is noteworthy that Cheney integrated students' interpersonal, affective, cognitive, and biological strengths into the action plan.

Theme 3: Inclusion

School inclusion was most often addressed through collaborative action research studies. Schoen and Bullard (2002) and Visoky and Poe (2000) studied the impact of peer buddies as models. The integration of general education curriculum standards and individualized objectives through co-planning and co-teaching was explored in studies by Argyropoulos and Stamouli (2006), Dymond, Renzaglia, Rosenstein, Chun, Banks, Niswander, and Gilson (2006), Langerock (2000), and Mendez, Lacasa, and Matusov (2008). Salisbury, Wilson, and Palombaro examined the efficacy of inclusion. The inclusion studies featured intense collaboration between general and special educators and others, including university professionals. Children are likely to benefit from observing collaborative adults who blend individual talents to effectively solve problems, as exemplified in the following statement by a child in the Langerock study who learned to recognize the learning strengths of peers:

> I like what Mrs. Langerock and Mrs. Black does because it helps everybody and it makes us to know even more. If I wanted help on my spelling, I would go with "G." "G" knows how to spell a lot. If I need help to get ideas in what to write, I would go to "D." If I need help on inventing something I would go to "S." If I needed help drawing something, I would go "W." (p. 33)

Sen and Goldbart (2005), a study on community inclusion, was the only identified critical action research study on children with disabilities. This study was conducted to identify children with disabilities living in legal and illegal slums in Kolkata, India, and to follow identification with family-based services. Collaborating agency professionals employed the use of trusted community members to better understand contextual barriers in the slums. They identified 25 children with disabilities, with 90% of their families reporting no prior access to educational services or adapted equipment. Services were based on family values and in a time frame that was respectful of the mothers' caregiving demands. This study, which was highly respectful of local context and values, demonstrated the feasibility of community-based models for identification, service provision, and improved community inclusion in high poverty regions.

Theme 4: Amplifying the Voices of Children with Disabilities

The theme of amplifying voice includes studies that made an explicit effort to draw out the voices of children (such as Richter, 1997, and Brookhart et al., 2004, discussed above), self-determination studies, and participatory action research studies. Self-determination involves taking actions to be the primary causal agent in one's life (Wehmeyer, 2005). Jones (2006) and Rose, Fletcher, and Goodwin (1999) engaged in multiple cycle action research to improve the self-determination skills of adolescents with disabilities. Both studies concluded that instruction of self-determination must begin when children are young, with gradually increased expectations for participation.

Photovoice, a research methodology rooted in feminist theory, Freire's critical education approach, and participatory documentary photography (Jurkowski, 2008), has been applied in participatory action research studies with both children and adults with disabilities. Central tenets of this method are that participants identify issues of importance and potential solutions. These participant responsibilities are fulfilled through the photovoice process that includes the act of taking photographs (on an identified topic or issue), followed by subsequent discussions about the ideas represented in the photographs. Participant control of the photographic experience is essential to capturing the participant's reality.

Carnahan (2006) applied photovoice methodology in a two-phase study that examined teachers' experiences (Phase I) and students' experiences (Phase II) of inclusion. Carnahan discovered that photovoice was effective in facilitating interactions between children with autism and their peers without disabilities. Further, joint attention and engagement improved in children with autism when interactions were focused around photographs about their preferred topics. These students learned that common interests transcend the presence or absence of disability. Carnahan concluded, "Photovoice can be used with teachers in reflection on their practice in inclusion and with students as a strategy to increase membership in the classroom community" (p. 49). Participatory action research studies conducted with adults may suggest fruitful topics and methods of research that may be applied to children and young adults with disabilities.

EXTENDING THE LITERATURE TO
ADDITIONAL ISSUES OF SOCIAL JUSTICE

Children and young adults with disabilities face a host of complex social justice issues, including stigmatization, segregation, limited access to the general education curriculum, vocational tracking, and the probability of adult poverty. Many of the studies discussed above shared the goal of improving learning outcomes for children with disabilities. Improved learning outcomes can result in improved life opportunities, which is the goal of research with an emphasis on social justice. This section will demonstrate that action research can be applied to address complex social justice issues for many children, by focusing on just one issue, disproportionality. A brief orientation to the literature on disproportionality is followed by suggestions for classroom, collaborative, critical, and participatory action research on this problem.

The Problem of Disproportionality

Disproportionality, the over- and underrepresentation of children in special education because of a characteristic such as race or gender, impacts children who have already been identified with a disability and those who may experience wrongful identification. Disproportionality does not occur across all categories of special education. Instead it plagues only the subjective categories, those that are commonly called the *judgmental categories* of special education, including mild intellectual disability, emotional disturbance, and learning disability (O'Connor & Fernandez, 2006).

Gender-related disproportionality research addresses the overrepresentation of boys and the underrepresentation of girls in special education. The biological advantage of females, higher activity levels in males, and teacher referral bias have been hypothesized to contribute to the overrepresentation of boys in special education (Wehmeyer & Schwartz, 2001). Girls tend to express emotional problems passively, resulting in underidentification of emotional disturbances (Arms, Bickett, & Graf, 2008). Girls with intellectual disability are identified at an older age and with a lower IQ than boys at the time of identification (Wehmeyer & Schwartz, 2001), suggesting that American society may be more accepting of lower performance in girls (Kratovil & Bailey, 2001). Gender equity does not mean that equal numbers of males and females should be identified for special education, but that both genders experience "full and nondiscriminatory identification under IDEA [Individuals with Disabilities Education Act]" (Coutinho & Oswald, 2005, p. 14).

While researchers agree that poverty and race both contribute to disproportionality in special education, there is disagreement about the relative contribution of each (Skiba, Poloni-Staudinger, Simmons, Feggins-Azzia, & Chung, 2005). Poor children are more likely to attend poorly resourced schools with teachers who are not as well qualified, and they are more likely to be tracked out of the most academically challenging programs, putting them at risk for eventual identification of a mild disability (Harris III, Brown, Ford, & Richardson, 2004; Rueda & Windmueller, 2006; Skiba, Simmons, Ritter, Gibb, Rausch, Cuadrado, & Chung, 2008).

African American and Native American children are overrepresented in special education, while Latino and Asian children are underrepresented (Artiles & Bal, 2008; Beratan, 2008; Grossman, 1995). Immigrants without a written language and nonvoluntary immigrants are at higher risk for identification of a disability, as are children from cultures that emphasize familism (Grossman, 1995; Harris III et al., 2004). Inequities extend beyond identification to service provision and placement. Minority children are more likely to receive fewer related services (therapies and consultation) and they are more likely to be placed in a more restrictive setting than identified white children (Artiles & Bal, 2008).

Numerous explanations and causes for the overrepresentation of children from minority racial and ethnic groups have been proposed in the literature, including poverty (and associated influences of housing, neighborhood instability, and lack of health care), low achievement (which coalesces with poverty, tracking, and unequal distribution of educational resources), assessment bias (test and examiner), pre-referral and referral problems, mismatch of teacher and student cultures (which may lead to misinterpretation of behavioral styles), racism, classism, cultural reproduction, and the failure of educational legislation to address power inequities (Harris III et al., 2004; O'Connor & Fernandez, 2006; Skiba et al., 2008; Skiba, Simmons, Ritter, Kohler, Henderson, & Wu, 2006).

Applying Classroom Action Research to the Problem of Disproportionality

Although disproportionality is a very complex and systemic problem with profound social and political implications, teachers can make a difference at the classroom level. The following example is used to illustrate how a novice teacher might apply classroom action research to the problem of disproportionality.

Ms. Emily Ward, a 1st-year third-grade teacher, is concerned about the practice of ability grouping in her school, and especially about its effects on early reading achievement. Given her 1st-year status and the lack of time for collaboration in her school, Ms. Ward selects a topic that she can reasonably address. She frames her topic into this broad action research question: *What effect does ability grouping have on student learning?* In her preliminary review of the literature, Ms. Ward discovers research evidence that ability grouping (including tracking) contributes to low achievement in students from some minority groups (Harris III et al., 2004). Ms. Ward decides to engage in journal-writing to examine her own beliefs and biases and how they contribute to her decisions about student grouping. In keeping with O'Hanlon's (2003) suggestions for journal entry headings, she will record research evidence including critical incidents, her ideas and reflections, actions planned and actions taken, and student academic and affective responses.

After reviewing the literature, journaling, examining academic performance data, and a few brief conversations with teacher colleagues, Ms. Ward decides that she wants to eliminate ability grouping for the rest of the school year. She decides to continue the practice of forming small groups of students (to increase one-on-one teacher attention and feedback) but she will group heterogeneously for some classroom lessons and by student interest for special projects. Her action research question has now become: *What happens when I eliminate ability grouping in my classroom?* She will continue to journal, refine her literature review, and examine student work for evidence of the efficacy of her new practice. If her new forms of grouping are efficacious, she will share her results with teachers in her school. If not, she will consider additional action research cycles.

Applying Collaborative Action Research to the Problem of Disproportionality

Collaborative action research in education occurs when teachers co-research topics of concern with others, such as related service professionals, university professionals, and consultants. Reading difficulties and behavioral issues are at the root of most special education referrals (Utley, Obiakor, & Kozleski, 2005), drawing attention to the need for effective reading instruction as well as an examination of the impact of school discipline codes on referrals for special education. A district could address concerns about reading achievement and instruction by implementing Response to Intervention (RTI). RTI is both a form of dynamic assessment and an instructional design that provides services to all children, thus eliminating the need to first identify a disability (Murawski & Hughes, 2009). Tier I supports are agreed upon instructional practices to implement with all children in general education. A district's action plan could include additional learning opportunities for general educators to become more knowledgeable about Tier I interventions. Since Tier II and Tier III supports are more individualized, the general educators, reading specialists, and special educators would collaborate to select appropriate instructional approaches, materials, and strategies to meet the needs of each student. The faculty, administration, and perhaps outside specialists would also consider procedural issues to enhance the effectiveness of the RTI teams. Like any pre-referral team, the success of RTI is related to the timing of the request for special assistance (not waiting too long), openness of the general educator to the team's suggestions, and the knowledge and skills of the RTI team members, especially their ability to generate new solutions (Skiba et al., 2006). Throughout the process, administrators would support effective intervention for all students by creating more time and greater rewards for collaboration with a focus on student learning.

Applying Critical Action Research to the Problem of Disproportionality

Critical action research would be especially appropriate when addressing disproportionality at the district level. Such an effort requires the formation of a community of inquiry that seeks and authentically includes input from community members who hold views that may be in opposition to the dominant view of school professionals. Here are some action research questions that would be suitable for critical action research on disproportionality at the district level:

- What are the possible causes for under- and overrepresentation in special education by gender, race, and ethnicity in our district?
- How can our school (or district) reduce the overrepresentation of minorities (or a specific minority group) identified with an emotional disturbance?
- How can we identify and implement the support of culture brokers to increase the cultural competence of our professional faculty and staff?
- What role can parents play in developing a more culturally sensitive districtwide discipline code?

Applying Participatory Action Research to the Problem of Disproportionality

In participatory action research, the participants assume co-researcher roles. Self-determination and self-advocacy are central to any participatory action research study (Bruyere, 1993; Porter & Lacey, 2005). Given that school suspensions and expulsions are highly predictive of identification for special education services (Skiba, Poloni-Staudinger, Simmons,

Feggins-Azzia, & Chung, 2005), a district might choose to study how the school discipline code impacts referrals for special education. The following questions (and subquestions) would be appropriate to such an effort:

- How is the current discipline code being implemented across schools (and grade levels) in our district?
- What evidence can we find to support the allegation that students in some minority groups are receiving harsher discipline for the same infractions?
- How can we include secondary students in the development of our school/district discipline code? How would they be selected?

Secondary students who are participants/co-researchers in the study could serve as data collectors to answer the above questions. They could interview peers to gain input from various racial and ethnic groups. They might also serve on focus groups to examine the themes adults generate from various data sources such as interviews and surveys. The district might also decide to implement a school discipline committee with hearing procedures that could include several student representatives elected by their fellow students. Finally, the participants could participate in evaluating the positive and negative outcomes of student participation in participatory action research on discipline.

Classroom, collaborative, critical, and participatory action research each hold an important place in addressing the challenges faced by children with disabilities and those who are risk for identification. Large-scale efforts that integrate the application of the four types of action research may be most effective in addressing pervasive and systemic issues of social justice that are grounded in long-standing, deeply rooted prejudices. This chapter has provided background information on types of action research, a brief discussion of existing action research studies in special education, and suggestions for applying action research to social justice issues. Chapter 3 builds on this knowledge by explicitly addressing how to conduct action research.

REFERENCES

Argyropoulos, V., & Stamouli, M. (2006). A collaborative action research project in an inclusive setting: Assisting a blind student. *British Journal of Visual Impairment, 24*(3), 128–134.
Arms, E., Bickett, J., & Graf, V. (2008). Gender bias and imbalance: Girls in U.S. special education programmes. *Gender and Education, 20*(4), 349–359.

Artiles, A. J., & Bal, A. (2008). The next generation of disproportionality research: Toward a comparative model in the study of equity in ability differences. *Journal of Special Education, 42*(1), 4–14.

Balcazar, F. E., Keys, C. B., Kaplan, D. L., & Suarez-Balcazar, Y. (1998). Participatory action research and people with disabilities: Principles and challenges. *Canadian Journal of Rehabilitation, 12*(2), 105–112.

Barnes, C. (2002). "Emancipatory disability research": Project or process? *Journal of Research in Special Educational Needs, 2*(1), 1–8.

Beratan, G. D. (2008). The song remains the same: Transposition and the disproportionate representation of minority students in special education. *Race, Ethnicity and Education, 11*, 337–354.

Brookhart, S. M., Andolina, M., Zuza, M., & Furman, R. (2004). Minute math: An action research study of student self-assessment. *Educational Studies in Mathematics, 57*, 213–227.

Bruyere, S. M. (1993). Participatory action research: Overview and implications for family members of persons with disabilities. *Journal of Vocational Rehabilitation, 3*(2), 62–68.

Capobianco, S. L., Lincoln, S., Canuel-Browne, D., & Trimarchi, R. (2006). Examining the experiences of three generations of teacher researchers through collaborative science teacher inquiry. *Teacher Education Quarterly, 33*(3), 61–78.

Carnahan, C. (2006). Photovoice: Engaging children with autism and their teachers. *TEACHING Exceptional Children, 39*(2), 44–50.

Cheney, D. (1998). Using action research as a collaborative process to enhance educators' and families' knowledge and skills for youth with emotional or behavioral disorders. *Preventing School Failure, 42*(2), 88–93.

Coutinho, M. J., & Oswald, D. P. (2005). State variation in gender disproportionality in special education: Findings and recommendations. *Remedial and Special Education, 26*(1), 7–15.

Dymond, S. K., Renzaglia, A., Rosenstein, A., Chun, E. J., Banks, R. A., Niswander, V., & Gilson, C. L. (2006). Using a participatory action research approach to create a universally designed high school science course: A case study. *Research and Practice for Persons with Severe Disabilities (RPSD), 31*(4), 293–308

Falk-Ross, F. F. (2000). Finding the right words: A case study in classroom-based language and literacy support. *Research in the Teaching of English, 34*, 499–531.

Gilbert, T. (2004). Involving people with learning disabilities in research: Issues and possibilities. *Health and Social Care in the Community, 12*(4), 298–308.

Grossman, H. (1995). *Special education in a diverse society.* Boston: Allyn and Bacon.

Harris III, J. J., Brown, E. L., Ford, D. Y., & Richardson, J. W. (2004). African Americans and multicultural education: A proposed remedy for disproportionate special education placement and underinclusion in gifted education. *Education and Urban Society, 36*(3), 304–341.

Hendricks, C. (2009). Improving schools through action research: A comprehensive guide for educators (2nd ed.). Upper Saddle River, NJ: Pearson.

Hobson, D. (2001). Learning with each other: Collaboration in teacher research. In G. Burnaford, J. Fischer, & D. Hobson (Eds.), *Teachers doing research: The power of action through inquiry* (2nd ed.). Mahwah, NJ: Erlbaum, (pp. 173–192).

Horner, R. H., & Carr, E. G. (1997). Behavioral support for students with severe disabilities: Functional assessment and comprehensive intervention. *The Journal of Special Education, 31*, 84–104.

Jones, M. (2006). Teaching self-determination: Empowered teachers, empowered students. *TEACHING Exceptional Children, 39*(1), 12–17.

Jurkowski, J. M. (2008). Photovoice as participatory action research tool for engaging people with intellectual disabilities in research and program development. *Intellectual and Developmental Disabilities, 46*(1), 1–11.

Kemmis, S., & McTaggart, R. (2005). Participatory action research: Communicative action and the public sphere. In N. K. Denzin & Y. S. Lincoln (Eds), *The Sage handbook of qualitative research.* (3rd ed.) (pp. 559–602). Thousand Oaks, CA: Sage.

Kratovil, J., & Bailey, S. M. (2001). Sex equity and disabled students. *Theory into Practice, XXV*(4), 250–256.

Langerock, N. L. (2000). A passion for action research. *TEACHING Exceptional Children, 33*(2), 26–32.

Marchand-Martella, N., Martella, R. C., Orlob, M., & Ebey, T. (2000). Conducting action research in a rural high school setting using peers as corrective reading. *Rural Special Education Quarterly, 19*(2), 20–30.

Mendez, L., Lacasa, P., & Matusov, E. (2008). Transcending the zone of learning disability: Learning in contexts for everyday life. *European Journal of Special Needs Education, 23*(1), 63–73.

Moni, K. B., Jobling, A., & van Kraayenoord, C. E. (2007). "They're a lot cleverer than I thought": Challenging perceptions of disability support as they tutor in an adult literacy program. *International Journal of Lifelong Education, 26*(4), 439–459.

Morgan, M. F., & Moni, K. B. (2008). Meeting the challenge of limited literacy resources for adolescents and adults with intellectual disabilities. *The British Journal of Special Education, 35*(2), 92–101.

Mortensen, S. (2002). Action research on cognitive rescaling. *Journal of Special Education Technology, 17*(4), 53–58.

Murawski, W. W., & Hughes, C. E. (2009). Response to intervention, collaboration, and co-teaching: A logical combination for successful systemic change. *Preventing School Failure, 53*(4), 267–277.

O'Connor, C., & Fernandez, S. D. (2006). Race, class, and disproportionality: Reevaluating the relationship between poverty and special education placement. *Educational Researcher, 35*(6), 6–11.

O'Hanlon, C. (2003). *Educational inclusion as action research: An interpretive discourse.* Maidenhead, UK: Open University Press.

Osborn, J., Freeman, A., Burley, M., Wilson, R., Jones, E., & Rychener, S. (2007). Effect of tutoring on reading achievement for students with cognitive disabilities, specific learning disabilities, and students receiving Title I services. *Education and Training in Developmental Disabilities, 42*(4), 467–474.

Park, H-S., Meyer, L., & Goetz, L. (1998). Introduction to the special series on participatory action research. *Journal of the Association for Persons with Severe Handicaps, 23*(3), 163–164.

Pine, G. J. (2009). *Teacher action research: Building knowledge democracies.* Los Angeles: Sage.

Porter, J., & Lacey, P. (2005). *Researching learning difficulties: A guide for practitioners.* London: Paul Chapman.

Richter, S. E. (1997). Using portfolios as an additional means of assessing written language in a special education classroom. *Teaching and Change, 5*(1), 58–70.

Rose, R., Fletcher, W., & Goodwin, G. (1999). Pupils with severe learning difficulties as personal target setters. *British Journal of Special Education, 26*(4), 206–212.

Rueda, R., & Windmueller, M. P. (2006). English language learners, LD, and overrepresentation. *Journal of Learning Disabilities, 39*(2), 99–107.

Salisbury, C. L., Wilson, L. I., & Palombaro, M. M. (1998). Promoting inclusive schooling practice through practitioner directed inquiry. *Journal of the Association for Persons with Severe Handicaps, 23*(3), 223–237.

Sample, P. L. (1996). Beginnings: Participatory action research and adults with developmental disabilities. *Disability & Society, 11*(3), 317–332.

Schoen, S. F., & Bullard, M. (2002). Action research during recess: A time for children with autism to play and learn. *TEACHING Exceptional Children, 35*(1), 36–39.

Schoen, S. F., & Nolen, J. (2004). Action research: Decreasing acting-out behavior and increasing learning. *TEACHING Exceptional Children, 37*(1), 26–29.

Schoen, S. F., & Schoen, A. A. (2003). Action research in the classroom: Assisting a linguistically different learner with special needs. *Teaching Exceptional Children, 35*(3), 16–21.

Schoen, S. F., & Thomas, R. (2006). Altering the inappropriate comments of a student with multiple disabilities. *Journal of Instructional Psychology, 33*(1), 75–79.

Sen, R., & Goldbart, J. (2005). Partnership in action: introducing family-based intervention for children with disability in urban slums of Kolkata, India. *International Journal of Disability, Development, and Education, 52*(4), 275–311.

Skiba, R. J., Poloni-Staudinger, L., Simmons, A. B., Feggins-Azzia, L. R., & Chung, C-G. (2005). Unproven links: Can poverty explain ethnic disproportionality in special education? *The Journal of Special Education, 39*(3), 130–144.

Skiba, R. J., Simmons, A. B., Ritter, S., Gibb, A. C., Rausch, M. K., Cuadrado, J., & Chung, C-G. (2008). Achieving equity in special education: History, status, and current challenges. *Exceptional Children, 72*(3), 264–288.

Skiba, R., Simmons, A., Ritter, S., Kohler, K., Henderson, M., & Wu, T. (2006). The context of minority disproportionality: Practitioner perspectives on special education referral. *Teachers College Record, 108*(7), 1424–1459.

Stevens, K. B., Slaton, D. B., & Bunney, S. (1992). A collaborative research effort between public school and university faculty members. *Teacher Education and Special Education, 15*(1), 1–8.

Utley, C. A., Obiakor, F. E., & Kozleski, E. B. (2005). Overrepresentation of culturally and linguistically diverse students in special education in urban schools: A research synthesis. In J. Flood & P. L. Anders (Eds.), *Literacy development of students in urban schools: Research and policy* (pp. 314–344). Newark, DE: International Reading Association.

Visoky, A. M., & Poe, B. D. (2000). Can preschoolers be effective peer models? *Teaching Exceptional Children, 33*(2), 68–73.

Walmsley, J. (2001). Normalisation, emancipatory disability research from theory to practice. In C. Barnes & G. Mercer (Eds.), *Doing disability research* (pp. 32–48). Leeds, U.K.: The Disability Press.

Wansart, W. L. (1995). Teaching as a way of knowing: Observing and responding to students' abilities. *Remedial and Special Education, 16*(3), 166–177.

Ward, K., & Trigler, S. (2001). Reflections on participatory action research with people who have developmental disabilities. *Mental Retardation, 39*(1), 57–59.

Welch, M., & Chisholm, K. (1994). Action research as a tool for preparing specialists to use strategic interventions in educational partnerships. *Teacher Education and Special Education, 17*(4), 269–279.

Wehmeyer, M. L. (2005). Self-determination and individuals with severe disabilities: Reexamining meanings and misinterpretations. *Research & Practice for Persons with Severe Disabilities, 30,* 113–120.

Wehmeyer, M. L., & Schwartz, M. (2001). Research on gender bias in special education services. In H. Rousso & M. L. Wehmeyer (Eds.), *Double jeopardy: Addressing gender equity in special education* (pp. 271–288). Albany: State University of New York Press.

3

Basic Principles for Conducting Action Research

Gerald J. Pine and Susan M. Bruce

"Action research takes place in a context of discovery and invention as opposed to a context of verification. Discovery and invention, the main business of human science has little to do with experimental designs. What one does to discover and invent a new way of teaching is a completely separate activity from the strict procedures of classical experimental design" (Pine, 2009, p. 236). Although action research does not follow a strict linear step-by-step structure, the following research phases (which may be revisited multiple times across multiple cycles of action and reflection) serve as a general guide:

- Identify the inquiry topic.
- Frame the research question.
- Develop the theoretical framework.
- Develop the research plan.
- Collect, organize, and analyze data.
- Draw conclusions, find meaning.
- Share/report findings.
(Falk-Ross & Cuevas, 2008; McNiff, Lomax, & Whitehead, 2006)

IDENTIFYING THE INQUIRY TOPIC

By studying life in the natural setting of the classroom, by looking closely for patterns in the intricacies of classroom life, by closely observing authentic events in teaching and learning situations, the classroom teacher can identify a research question that will evoke personal passion and energy. Passion is integral to doing action research and can be a resource for identifying a suitable research topic. Teachers and related service professionals may feel passionate about helping one child, improving the curriculum, improving implementation of a new instructional approach or intervention, examining the match/mismatch between professional beliefs and actual daily practice, or identifying a role to address an issue of social justice (Dana & Yendol-Hoppy, 2008). One's passions, the issues that one cares about the most, should drive the selection of the research topic.

The questions teachers regularly pose about teaching and learning will propel them toward research topics (Hansen, 1997). Meaningful research topics can emerge from conversations with colleagues, the professional literature, examination of professional journal entries to identify patterns of teacher/student behavior, dissonance between teaching intentions and outcomes, curiosity about a student's work, and problematic learning situations in the classroom. Teachers may seek to explain why a particular strategy has been successful or to study the implementation of a new teaching strategy. Teachers may decide to study an ambiguous and puzzling classroom management concern, the processes and products of a group curriculum project, or student-centered learning activities, or test a particular theory and its associated practices in the classroom.

Everyday professional journals or field notes may be the source of an action research topic. Field notes may be (1) general notes on the classroom, (2) notes on a specific issue, (3) descriptions of one child's learning, or (4) notes on one's own development as a teacher or related service professional (Hopkins, 2002). Cindy Meyers (Goswami & Stillman, 1987, p. 3) discusses how the process of research in her classroom is clarified and informed by her field notes:

> Every year when I start research by keeping field notes, I keep thinking that this is an exercise, and I'm just writing down what's happening and I'm not getting anything out of it. It seems like a bland kind of thing. But when I keep doing that, all of a sudden I'll hear the kids say something that shows they've changed in some way, And I'll put that down too. And then things start to pull together. It's almost like the field notes that I keep and through what I see happening— out of those field notes—the classroom becomes more alive.

Sometimes it helps to use a variety of question stems as starting points to identify an issue to research. A few examples follow:

> I would like to improve _____.
> I want to learn more about _____.
> I am really concerned about _____.
> What happens to student learning in my classroom
>   when I _____?
> How can I implement _____?
>   (Caro-Bruce, 2000)

The potential number of research topics that are inherent in the context of the classroom, in the context of teaching, and in the context of learning are almost infinite. Teachers engage in as many as 1,000 interpersonal interactions within a school day (Jackson, 1968). These interactions may be the source of the research topic, or they may help to clarify the topic. Identifying a good research question from the many possibilities requires reflection, observation, conversation, and deep thinking about the complexities of classroom life.

FROM INQUIRY TOPIC TO FRAMING THE RESEARCH QUESTION

In one's eagerness to begin a research study, sometimes there is a tendency to try to state the question as soon as possible. It is advisable not to hurry the question. Identifying the research topic and framing the research question should be done carefully after contemplating many different angles. Reflection about teaching and learning will cause ideas to percolate. It may be helpful to brainstorm research questions and talk them over with colleagues. The questions should emerge over time until the teacher feels ready to frame the question that will guide the inquiry.

A Good Classroom Action Research Question

A good classroom action research question should be meaningful and important to the teacher or related service professional. It should engage one's passion, energy, and commitment. It should be important to personal and professional growth. A good research question is manageable and within one's sphere of influence, something that can be reasonably accomplished.

A good research question should be important for learners. A study founded on a good research question benefits students by informing teaching and the curriculum and by providing the professional(s) with new insights about students and their learning. A good research question leads to taking an action to improve a teaching/learning situation. Even in those situations in which the goal of the research is to gain deeper knowledge and understanding of a student, such as in a case study or a descriptive review, the ultimate goal of such acquired knowledge and understanding is the improvement of teaching and the advancement of student learning.

A good research question is sufficiently open ended to facilitate meaningful exploration, to allow new possibilities to emerge (Hubbard & Power, 1993). Open-ended questions cannot be answered with a simple "yes" or "no." Responding to the more open-ended research question will more often than not generate multiple directions and further research questions.

The research question should be jargon-free and absent of value-laden terms. Questions beginning with "what," "why," or "how" are usually broader and get at explanations, relationships, and reasons. Carol Avery, a teacher researcher, discusses how framing her question with "what," "how," and "why" changed her way of seeing children:

> As a teacher researcher I became a learner in the classroom concerned with what my students were learning and how they were learning. I experienced the classroom as a collaborative venture and examined not only how I functioned but also how we worked together and why strategies did or did not work. Asking questions of how and why led the way for me to delve into children's individual learning patterns, to see children in the context of their unique situations, and to understand and value the richness of their differences. I developed a responsive mode of teaching; I became more flexible in dealing with the children. (1990, p. 37)

A good research question is authentic because the teacher owns it. Teacher researchers are encouraged to use the personal pronouns "I" or "we" and phrases such as "in my classroom" or "in our school" in the statement of the research question. When the teacher owns the question, he/she is more likely to feel invested in the research. In using personal pronouns, the teacher claims personal ownership of the question and acknowledges the subjectivity that exists in all research (Pine, 2009). The rationale for the inclusion of the personal pronoun is eloquently stated by McNiff, Lomax, and Whitehead (2006, p. 17):

How do "I" fit into the research?
- I am the subject and object of the research.
- I take responsibility for my own actions.
- I own my claims and judgments.
- I am the author of my own research accounts.

How do "I" fit into the action?
- by seeing my own practice as the central focus of my research through critical reflection and self study
- by encouraging others to participate in a negotiated definition of shared practices
- by showing respect for other ways of doing things
- by showing humility and exposing my vulnerability
- by being open to argument
- by being willing to accept that I could be wrong
- by owning my mistakes
- by standing my ground when my principles are at stake.

The personal relationship with our research extends beyond the "I" or the "we" in the question, as described by Ellis, a teacher researcher:

> Conducting research makes you take the time to think about what you're doing and to kind of chart the course according to what happens and what you notice and the reactions or responses that your kids have. So it's like having an out of body experience because I'm looking at myself in the classroom from outside myself. (Rogers, 2004a, p. 69)

It is important to remember that the first question that propels an action research study may change as the research is under way. The recursive, iterative, and spiraling nature of action research suggests that a research question may change and be refined as new data and issues surface in the research study. Carol Battaglia (1995), a classroom teacher, offers this advice on changing questions:

> Change questions! The questions I ask regarding my practice keep changing. Action research involves refining questions until you feel you have landed upon the right ones. I now see that the way you frame questions will, inevitably, determine the methodology you plan to study them. Differentiated solutions and subsequent understandings will be generated by the way questions are posed. . . . Action research is so much a matter of "seeing" that it is a good idea, I found, to develop a little intellectual schizophrenia. Be your own arbiter. Wear another hat, use a different lens, try to unpack your thinking in a different way. . . . Don't fall in love with an idea when it is the only one you have. Have the courage to kiss them goodbye. (p. 91)

DEVELOPING THE THEORETICAL FRAMEWORK

The development of the theoretical framework will include a review of the literature. Information sources for the literature review are varied and may include books; professional journals; official government publications; research reports issued by foundations, professional organizations, and government agencies; theses and dissertations; school documents; assessment tools; curricula; and Internet resources. (For additional information about using the Internet as a teaching and information resource see Green, Brown, & Robinson, 2008; Nelson, 2008; and Richardson, 2006). A good-quality literature review will establish what has been done and what needs to be done. The literature review supports the teacher to develop a conceptual framework; understand the problem of interest; identify areas of controversy in the research; establish and define the social, educational, cultural, and historical contexts of the problem or question; develop the research design and methodology; and provide a check for testing later findings and conclusions (Hart, 1998).

Because of the recursive, iterative, spiraling, and cyclical nature of action research, it is imperative to recognize that as new questions and issues emerge, it will become necessary to read in different and new literature than what had been originally planned. Often, the process of organizing and analyzing data causes one to return to examine additional literature. In action research, then, the literature review can be considered not as a static collection of literature but rather as an evolving, shifting, and changing body of work that shares a reciprocal relationship with the dynamics of the action research process. The iterative and recursive nature of the research affects the literature review, and the changing literature review affects the conduct and direction of the research.

Based on their experience working with action researchers over the years, Holly, Arhar, and Kasten (2005, pp. 114–115) make the following suggestions on the conduct of a literature review:

- Read broadly and generally at first, then read more narrowly.
- When you are researching a novel topic that seems to have few resources, look for related topics and then synthesize them.
- Consult primary resources where possible . . . The rule of thumb is to use as many primary resources as is possible and feasible, and to check secondary sources to make sure that the information quoted is accurate.
- Ask for help. A few well-placed questions to a librarian, media specialist, and colleagues can be helpful.
- Read enough to get started, but not so much that you become too exhausted to conduct your study.
- Read with a critical eye . . . What are the theories, assumptions, and frameworks of the researchers? Are they plausible? Are they consistent with what you know? What is explained? What is left for interpretation?

While reading the literature, it may be helpful to highlight, underline, write in the margins, or use sticky notes to support the identification of big ideas or themes. It may be helpful to record summary notes and then to read those notes multiple times to support the identification of emerging themes that can be recorded in the margins. Later, a visual representation (such as a drawing or chart) can be developed to depict how the themes connect to the research study (Falk & Blumenreich, 2005). These efforts will support the identification of theories, instructional approaches, instructional strategies, and instructional content that are relevant to the action research study.

DEVELOPING THE
ACTION RESEARCH PLAN

After completing the first examination of the literature, it is time to develop the research plan. In this book, we emphasize the case study design (individual, classroom, or school), but other research designs are suitable to the philosophy of action research. The research design, including the data sources selected, must fit the question posed. It is important to keep the study small and focused and to be realistic about what can be accomplished. Key elements for the conduct of action research include: careful planning, a timeline for data collection, involvement of others (such as a critical friend who can discuss your research), adherence to ethical research practices, and keeping teacher learning as part of the research focus (McNiff & Whitehead, 2002).

Identifying Data Sources

A good action research plan will help participants think through important questions for data gathering, facilitate coordination of resources and timelines so that data are gathered by design rather than by chance, and bring clarity so that data are collected correctly the first time. The following questions can guide decision-making about the data sources (selection, organization, and analysis):

- Why am I collecting the data?
- How are the data related to the research question?
- What will the data tell me about the research problem?
- What kind of data will yield the best information? What counts as data?
- What data will I collect? How much data will I collect? Will data be easy or difficult to collect?
- Who will be using the data? Who will be seeing the data?
- What data sources will I use to collect information?
- When will the data be collected?
- Who will collect the data?
- How will the data be collected and analyzed? How systematic will data collection be?
- How will the data be organized? How will the data be displayed?
- What criteria will be used to analyze the data?
- How will the data be recorded and shared?
- Where will the data be housed?

(Pine, 2009, p. 251)

There are innumerable data sources in schools, including the data that can be found in every classroom in any school. It may be helpful to collaboratively brainstorm data sources. Pine (2009) categorized the many and varied data sources as existing archival sources, conventional sources, and inventive sources. *Existing archival data sources* are those items currently available in the files or archives of the school or of individual staff members, including student grades, attendance patterns, individualized education plans (IEPs), number of referrals, retentions, number/percentage of students in special programs, standardized test results, school mission statements, staff development plans, meeting agendas, discipline records, and counseling service referrals. *Conventional data sources* are items that require communication, observation, or follow-up with members of the population, including interviews, surveys, checklists, number of books read, writing samples, variety of materials used, observations, and journals. *Inventive sources* are usually more creative, complex, and deep. We use these sources when we want even more in-depth or qualitatively different information than we can gain from existing and conventional sources. Inventive sources include authentic assessment, performance assessment, exhibits, portfolios, expositions, videotapes, photographs, and children's drawings.

The teacher or collaborative research team must consider how each data source will inform the research question. For example, a research question about one student's behavior might require the following data sources: teacher journal, behavior data sheet, parent survey, and sample student work. Multiple data sources inform a study from different vantage points.

Ethical Considerations

The action research study and plan should reflect ethical principles of research. Ethical research is guided by a respect for the participants, including considerations of the relative benefits and risks to the participants (Nolen & Putten, 2007). Informed consent, assent, and confidentiality are critical components of ethical research. Consent is appropriately informed when participants understand enough about the study to make a good decision about participation. The letter of permission or consent should include: (1) explanation of the research in layman's terms, (2) request to use student work, audiotapes, or videotapes of students (including specific uses), (3) explanation of how confidentiality will be ensured, (4) statement that participation is voluntary, will not involve harm, and that the participant has the right to withdraw from the study without penalty and at any time, (5) study risks and benefits, and

(6) researcher contact information so that participants or guardians may seek clarification about the research requirements (Hubbard & Power, 1999; McNiff & Whitehead, 2006; Mills, 2007). When an individual cannot consent (such as all minors and individuals with diminished capacity), procedures to determine assent (agreement to participate) must be included in the research plan. If a child refuses to participate or shows signs (including nonverbal signs) of anxiety that exceed what is typical for the child), one should seriously consider that the child is either not giving or is withdrawing assent. Confidentiality is another ethical principle that must be addressed in the research plan. This includes the handling of participant identity and information (such as the choice to use pseudonyms) and the storage of data so that it cannot be linked with the identities of the participants.

COLLECTING, ORGANIZING, AND ANALYZING DATA

The biggest challenge in conducting action research is to collect and analyze data while being in the midst of teaching. So in the process of implementing an intervention to improve student learning or to change teaching practices, the teacher must be mindful of the details that will make the intervention successful while at the same time exercising care in collecting and analyzing data that will determine the success of the intervention. Whatever data sources are used, it is important to collect data in an ongoing fashion. As one teacher researcher, Peter White (1998, p. 6), advises:

> I cannot stress too strongly the need to make sure that you are gathering all the data at the moment it is there. When I went back to check my field notes on the class time that I described in this essay, I discovered to my chagrin that I had not documented what I had written on the dry erase board. After the class left, I was tired and the next class was coming through the door, along with the instructor. I looked at the board, at all that was written, and thought, "I don't need to write that down. I'll remember. But, I didn't. . . . But, I've learned my lesson. Save as much documentation as possible. It will be valuable in the future."

The following suggestions may support the organization and analysis of data:

1. Organize and code data as they are collected, comparing new data with data collected and coded earlier. Organize the data based on what is being learned from the data.

2. Write continuously to document actions and ideas as they take place. Record thoughts about the data. The act of writing may reveal meaning and significance in the data. It may be necessary to rewrite the research question in response to what is being learned.

3. Look for patterns in the data coding. Review information after it is coded to determine frequencies of certain phenomena, emerging themes, or events of interest that seem particularly important to the research question. Determine the themes by reading and rereading the data. Key words or repetitive language and ideas may emerge in the data. These are helpful clues to the identification of themes. Some ideas may fit into more than one theme, and there may be subideas within themes.

4. Create a visual representation of the data collected. An idea map, a drawing, or a chart (using shapes and color to organize your ideas) are all possibilities to help one make sense of the data and to display a representation of the researcher's ideas.

5. The researcher must remain open to the data, to be influenced by it. Sometimes we are surprised by the data sources that provide the richest information. The data analysis period must be sufficiently long enough to allow the data to shape researcher thinking. Look for findings that are both similar to and contrary to the assumptions, findings, and theories uncovered in the literature review. Openness toward the data will allow the researcher to identify the need for additional cycles of action. Teacher learning and subsequent action cycles should be recorded to clarify the connections between data, reflection, and action.

6. Identify and state key findings. The findings should capture the story told by the data.

7. Share preliminary findings with colleagues who are critical friends. Explain your data interpretations. Consider your colleagues' interpretations and use them to clarify, broaden, and otherwise validate your findings.

(Depka, 2006; James, 1999; Madison Metropolitan School District Web site: Classroom Action Research; Pine, 2009; Power, 1996; Shea, Murray, & Harlin, 2005; Stainback & Stainback, 1988)

Always keep in mind that action research is a recursive, dynamic, and cyclical process of inquiry. These recommendations are not steps to be followed in a sequential manner. As data are collected and analyzed, it may be necessary to modify the research question. This may, in turn, lead to another cycle of data collection. This is all part of the process of recursion. In short, "Live with your data. Be a detective. Mull, contemplate, observe and inspect. Think about, through, and beyond" (Bateson as cited in Bochner, 1981, p. 76).

DRAWING CONCLUSIONS, FINDING MEANING

From the data analysis one needs to develop the findings and implications of the research for teaching and learning. It is not the data but the meanings that we apply to the data that are critical. However, it is important not to draw inferences from the data that the data will not support or to generalize the findings of the research beyond the study's parameters as defined in your research question. Engaging in dialogue with critical friends can help to unearth the meanings and conclusions of the study and their implications for practice. What story or stories do the data tell? Does the data analysis confirm or disconfirm the effectiveness of the action or intervention? Has the research question been answered, or are there more questions that have emerged? If there are significant differences between what the data say about the research question and what was expected, then these differences should be explored and viewed as rich opportunities for learning.

SHARING FINDINGS

Dissemination, or the sharing of research findings, is a critical phase of research. Dissemination may occur by sharing research with critical friends or a broader group of colleagues within the school, at a conference, or through publication. However research is shared, it is important to consider the audience and what they want to learn from it. Sagor (2005), Johnson (2008), and Mertler (2009) suggest that dissemination include the following: share information about researcher background and current context; explain the goal/focus of the study; and describe the research plan to accomplish the goal, the actions taken, the data collected (or a subset of the data depending on audience interest and need), what was learned, how actions were changed in response to data, plans for future action cycles or a new study, and time for questions and discussion. In discussing the study, it is imperative to delineate the limitations of the findings and of the research study. The findings should not be inadvertently overgeneralized, and one must be careful not to interject opinions that are not supported by the data. Through sharing the findings and research experiences, the teacher researcher may influence the thinking and actions of colleagues. Engaging in action research may even alter one's engagement in the larger school context, as described by Ms. Hermann (quoted in Rogers, 2004b):

> I was not as involved in my school before I became a teacher researcher. There was a certain confidence that I was able to get from knowing that I knew how to collect data, I knew how to analyze data, I knew how to share it with people. I was excited about what I was doing in my class. I really wanted to be able to share that with people. People on the teacher research team did get involved with the planning group because, once we had this knowledge, we wanted to be able to make a difference in our building. (p. 114)

EVALUATING THE ACTION RESEARCH STUDY

Evaluation is a phase of the research process that includes an examination of the development process and the results. This examination includes the identification of what went well, what didn't, and what could be done differently in a subsequent action research study. O'Hanlon (2003, p. 35) suggests the following quality indicators that can be used to guide the evaluation of action research studies:

- credibility, established by the voice of the researcher being made public;
- inclusion of the researcher's values, beliefs, and assumptions;
- clarity of the research question or issue, the purpose of the research, and its process;
- incorporation of revisions in the direction of the research and changes in practice resulting from it (action cycles);
- assurance that practical action strives to achieve educational aims;
- explicit connections made between the research and the learners to whom the educational aims are directed;
- demonstration of a self-critical stance toward practice and research;
- bringing multiple perspectives to the data and ensuring accuracy in its handling through self-checking;
- addressing an issue that is of interest to others in the educational community;
- presentation of sufficient and convincing evidence to support assertions and claims made in research reports or in practice;
- conclusions following directly from the evidence;

- transferability to other situations, i.e., something similar could be done by others;
- inclusion of new questions and insights that arise from the research;
- characterization of the work as unfinished, a continuing venture:
- provocation through the setting of challenges to others and oneself in the ideas presented;
- demonstration of the importance of the research as the justification for doing it.

APPLYING THE PRINCIPLES

This chapter provides basic guidance on how to conduct a classroom action research study. The reader may want to review the reference lists that follow each chapter for additional resources to support the conduct of action research. Chapters 5 through 8 of this text are examples of authentic classroom and collaborative action research studies that applied the basic principles for conducting research described in this chapter.

It seems most appropriate to close a discussion about the doing of educational action research with the words of a teacher researcher. In the following passage, Denise Dabish (2001) describes her action research experience:

> In the end, I feel I have learned a great deal more than the answer to my research question. I believe that by becoming a teacher researcher I have rediscovered my desire to teach and my quest for improving how I teach. When I think about the path I took to become a teacher researcher I am no longer scared of being a teacher who conducts research. I kept wondering how my research was going to take shape . . . I had to trust what I was doing was going to point me in the right direction. Now I know that simply starting with a question is all the information one needs to embark on an incredible journey of teacher discovery and research. Already I find myself wondering about what intriguing, important questions I will "live" next year as my students and I learn and grow together.

REFERENCES

Avery, C. (1990). Learning to research/researching to learn. In M. Olson (Ed.), *Opening the door to classroom research* (pp. 32–44). Newark, DE: International Reading Association.

Battaglia, C. (1995). Confused on a higher level about more important things.

In S. E. Nofke & R. B. Stevenson (Eds.), *Educational action research: Becoming practically critical* (pp. 74–93). New York: Teachers College Press.

Bochner, A. (1981). Forming warm ideas. In C. Wilder-Mott & J. Weakland (Eds.), *Rigor and imagination: Essays from the legacy of Gregory Bateson* (pp. 65–75). New York: Praeger.

Caro-Bruce, C. (2000). *Action research facilitator's handbook.* Oxford, OH: National Staff Development.

Dabish, D. (2001). From desks to quest: Understanding the process of teacher research. *Networks: An Online Journal for Teacher Research, 4*(2). Retrieved June 2008 from http://journals.library.wisc.edu/inddex.php/networks/article/view/37/42.

Dana, N. F., & Yendol-Hoppey, D. (2008). *The reflective educator's guide to classroom research.* Thousand Oaks, CA: Corwin Press.

Depka, E. (2006). *The data guidebook for teachers and leaders.* Thousand Oaks, CA: Corwin Press.

Falk, B., & Blumenreich, M. (2005). *The power of questions: A guide to teacher and student research.* Portsmouth, NH: Heinemann.

Falk-Ross, F. C., & Cuevas, P. D. (2008). Getting the big picture: An overview of the teacher research process. In C. Lassonde & S. E. Israel (Eds.), *Teachers taking action: A comprehensive guide to teacher research* (pp. 15–43). Newark, DE: International Reading Association.

Goswami, D., & Stillman, P. R. (1987). *Reclaiming the classroom: Teacher research as an agency for change.* Portsmouth, NH: Heinemann.

Green, T. D., Brown, A., & Robinson, L. (2008). *Making the most of the web in your classroom.* Thousand Oaks, CA: Corwin Press.

Hansen, J. (1997). Researchers in our own classrooms: What propels teacher researchers? In D. Leu, C. Kinzer, & K. Hinchman (Eds.), *Literacies for the 21st century: Research and practice* (pp. 1–14). Chicago: National Reading Conference.

Hart, C. (1998). *Doing a literature review: Releasing the social science imagination.* London: Sage.

Holly, M. L., Arhar, J., & Kasten, W. (2005). *Action research for teachers: Traveling the yellow brick road.* Upper Saddle River, NJ: Pearson/Prentice Hall.

Hopkins, D. (2002. *A teacher's guide to classroom research* (3rd ed.). Buckingham, UK: Open University Press.

Hubbard, R. S., & Power, B. M. (1993). Finding and framing a research question. In L. Patterson, C. M. Santa, K. G. Short, & K. Smith (Eds.), *Teachers are researchers: Reflection and action* (pp. 19–25). Newark, DE: International Reading Association.

Hubbard, R. S., & Power, B. M. (1999). *Living the questions: A guide for teacher-researchers.* York, ME: Stenhouse Publishers.

Jackson, P. W. (1968). *Life in classrooms.* New York: Holt, Rinehart and Winston.

James, P. (1999). Rewriting narratives of self: Reflections from an action research study. *Educational Action Research, 7*(1), 85–102.

Johnson, A. P. (2008). *A short guide to action research* (3rd ed.). Boston: Allyn & Bacon.

Madison Metropolitan School District. *Classroom action research.* Retrieved June 2, 2009, from the Madison Metropolitan School District Web site, http://www .madison.k12.wi.us/sod/car/carhomepage.html

McNiff, J., & Whitehead, J. (2006). *All you need to know about action research.* Thousand Oaks, CA: Sage.

McNiff, J., with Whitehead, J. (2002). *Action research: Principles and practices.* London: Routledge, Falmer/Taylor & Francis Group.

Mertler, C. A. (2009). *Action research: Teachers as researchers in the classroom.* (2nd ed.). Los Angeles: Sage.

Mills, G. E. (2007). *Action research: A guide for the teacher researcher* (3rd ed.). Upper Saddle River, NJ: Pearson Education.

Nelson, K. J. (2008). *Teaching in the digital age* (2nd ed.) Thousand Oaks, CA: Sage.

Nolen, A. L., & Putten, J. V. (2007). Action research in education: Addressing gaps in ethical principles and practices. *Educational Researcher, 36*(7), 401–407.

O'Hanlon, C. (2003). *Educational inclusion as action research: An interpretive discourse.* Berkshire, U.K.: Open University Press.

Pine, G. J. (2009). *Teacher action research: Building knowledge democracies.* Los Angeles: Sage.

Power, B. M. (1996). *Taking note: Improving your observational note-taking.* York, ME: Stenhouse.

Richardson, W. (2006). *Blogs, wikis, podcasts, and other powerful web tools for class-rooms.* Thousand Oaks, CA: Corwin Press.

Rogers, C. (2004a). Coming into focus: How teacher-researchers learn. In M. M. Mohr, C. Rogers, B. Sanford, M. A. Nocerino, M. S. MacLean, & S. Clawson, *Teacher research for better schools* (pp. 66–81). New York: Teachers College Press.

Rogers, C. (2004b). The leaven in the loaf: Teacher research knowledge in schools. In M. M. Mohr, C. Rogers, B. Sanford, M. A. Nocerino, M. S. MacLean, & S. Clawson, *Teacher research for better schools* (pp. 107–117). New York: Teachers College Press.

Sagor, R. (2005). *The action research guidebook: A four-step process for educators and school teams.* Thousand Oaks, CA: Corwin Press.

Shea, M., & Murray, R., & Harlin, R. (2005). *Drowning in data? How to collect, orga-nize, and document student performance.* Thousand Oaks, CA: Corwin Press.

Stainback, S., & Stainback, W. (1988). *Understanding and conducting qualitative research.* Reston, VA: Council for Exceptional Children.

White, P. (1998). Understanding prolepsis through teacher research. *Networks: An On-line Journal for Teacher Research, 1*(1). Retrieved September 2, 2008, from http://journals.library.wisc.edu/index.php/networks/index.

4

Reflection, Inquiry, and Action Research in Special Education Teacher Preparation Programs

Susan M. Bruce

Increasingly, teacher preparation programs include an action research component (Price, 2001) that requires teacher candidates to demonstrate reflection and inquiry about student learning and about their own development as teachers. The action research component is often situated within a larger focus on supporting candidates to become reflective practitioners. The first half of this chapter discusses how the concepts of reflection, inquiry stance, and action research are connected in teacher preparation. The second half of the chapter is devoted to sharing how two university special education teacher preparation programs prepare candidates to engage in action research couched within a broader emphasis on reflection and inquiry.

REFLECTION, INQUIRY, AND ACTION RESEARCH

"Teaching is a complex and dilemma-ridden endeavor, necessitating ongoing learning as well as the capacity to be reflective" (Cooper & Larrivee, 2006, p. 1). Reflection is a special kind of thinking that addresses a situation that causes doubt or perplexes one. For teachers, reflection occurs over a problem or question that emerges in the classroom. Reflection may occur at different levels of complexity, including (1) surface reflection (thinking about strategies and methods applied to accomplish established instructional goals), (2) pedagogical reflection (thinking deeply about educational goals and the connection between theory and practice), and (3) critical reflection (examining one's own assumptions, values, biases, ethics, and issues of social justice in the classroom, school, or larger community) (Cooper & Larrivee). Teacher reflection may be supported by technology, such as using word processing to record and organize thoughts, participating in listservs, organizing and analyzing data through software programs, and engaging in discourse at Web sites that share teacher action research (Hobson & Smolin, 2001).

The reflective teacher solves dilemmas while maintaining a keen awareness of his/her own assumptions, values, personal experiences, and institutional and cultural contexts. The reflective teacher takes responsibility for his/her own actions and participates in shaping curriculum development and school reform (Zeicher & Liston, 1996). Reflective practitioners apply an inquiry-based approach to teaching (Raisch, 1994), are open-minded to different points of view and to different forms of evidence, take responsibility for their actions, and eagerly seek opportunities to learn (Cooper & Larrivee, 2006; Dewey, 1916).

Preparation as a reflective practitioner begins in the teacher preparation program and continues after graduation. University field supervisors (of preservice candidates) and mentors (of novice in service teachers) can engage in reflective dialogue with the novice teacher, posing questions to encourage reflection and providing verbal and written feedback about practice. These dialogues support the teacher to move beyond thinking about the technical aspects of teaching. Schools can encourage novice teachers to engage in reflection by encouraging them to voice their ideas during staff meetings and by including them in a variety of school tasks, including school reform planning efforts (Pedro, 2006). Teacher candidates and novice teachers need opportunities to engage in problem solving and in oral and written reflection.

Within the teacher preparation program, service learning may be a fruitful area for engaging in reflection and in action research. Griffith (2005) conducted an action research study that examined the influence of service learning on the beliefs of preservice general and special educators about working with disadvantaged youth. The teacher candidates provided tutoring and participated in additional activities with children living in homeless shelters. They were encouraged to reflect upon these experiences by writing in a journal. The candidates then reviewed their journals to identify five lessons learned that would impact their future teaching. The following three themes emerged out of the lessons learned: factors that influence behavior and learning, traits of effective teachers, and challenging beliefs and practices. Examples of teacher candidate reflection, organized within these three themes, follow.

Factors that influence behavior and learning:
I have learned that family stress affects the way children learn. Children that have one parent with no job have a high level of stress. My job will be to listen attentively and offer hope to these children. Stress management will be vital to these children. (p. 287)

Traits of effective teachers:
A lot of positive reinforcement can help contribute to better behavior. This
has taught me that sincere positive reinforcement has an impact on students.
Just giving a student a high-five for doing good work can improve the mood
he is in. A little love and support can go a long way. (p. 287)

Challenging beliefs and practices:
I learned that students are often anxious to learn no matter what their socioeconomic status is. This means that every student in my class will be given an
equal opportunity to learn regardless of their economic situation. (p. 291)

These teacher candidates reflected upon their service experiences to construct the beginnings of who they intended to become as teachers.

Effective teachers know that inquiry into practice is a daily event.
"It's especially important that preservice teachers realize that the discovery is never complete; we are constantly learning throughout our careers
from our students, colleagues, and from our experiences" (Hobson, 2001,
p. 12). Preservice teacher preparation in inquiry must extend beyond
a single assignment (such as performing an action research study) to
preparation in *inquiry as stance* to support teacher candidates to construct deeply contextualized knowledge about teaching and learning.
These deep contextualized understandings hold the power to transform
teaching (Pine, 2009).

Cochran-Smith and Lytle (2009) define four central tenets of inquiry
stance: (1) a perspective of knowledge as being local expertise within
global contexts, (2) practice as the interaction of teaching, learning, and
leadership roles, (3) inquiry as stance occurs in the context of learning
communities, and (4) the primary purpose of teacher inquiry is to create
a just society. Thus, inquiry as stance is a way of knowing, a way of
being, and a theory of action that holds the power to transform learning
and teaching.

With three out of five special educators leaving the profession prior
to their 6th year of teaching, it is critical that we develop preparation
programs that are constructed on what we know about effective teaching. Hiebert, Morris, Berk, and Jansen (2007) proposed a framework for
preparing effective teachers. They suggested that in addition to mastering
subject matter knowledge and pedagogical knowledge, teacher candidates
must be prepared to analyze teaching in terms of student learning. The
authors suggest the following four skills as being essential to this process:
(1) establish outcomes for student learning, (2) assess student learning
outcomes, (3) generate hypotheses about student learning outcomes (why
they were or were not met), and (4) revise lessons based on the hypotheses. Teacher candidates who engage in action research with a focus on

student learning are working on the development of all four skills while still in a context where more knowledgeable others (such as the cooperating teacher and university field instructor) may scaffold their application of subject matter knowledge and pedagogical knowledge.

Teacher retention and excellence may also be addressed by preparing what Malone and Tulbert (1996) called the "centered teacher." Centered teachers are self-aware, have effective interpersonal skills, and engage in self-renewal. Action research is one form of self-renewal that allows teachers to further develop their self-awareness while engaging in collaboration with others. This self-awareness includes recognition of the influence of personal values, assumptions, and experiences on teaching. Centered teachers engage in action research, which improves their ability to solve problems in the classroom (Malone & Tulbert, 1996).

Reflection is integral to action research, which is situation-specific, highly contextualized inquiry (Rose & Grosvenor, 2001). Action research facilitates self-renewal as it breaks down the isolation experienced by teachers (Cooper & Larrivee, 2006; Raisch, 1994). Isolation can be particularly challenging for special educators in rural settings and those who teach children with low-incidence disabilities (Collins, Grisham-Brown, & Schuster, 1998). Preparing teachers who can conduct action research is important to supporting ongoing reflection and improvement in instruction that leads to improved student learning outcomes. Action research supports ongoing professional development, and it may also support the retention of special education teachers.

Pine (2009) recognized the role of action research in the ongoing professional development of teachers:

> Action research can be conceived as a form of professional development characterized as an ongoing process of systematic study in which teachers examine their own teaching and students' learning through descriptive reporting, purposeful conversation, collegial sharing, and critical reflection for the purpose of improving classroom practice. (p. 93)

By participating in the conceptualization and implementation of action research, teacher candidates construct their roles, including how they will approach dilemmas in the classroom and how they will think about student learning, content knowledge, and pedagogical knowledge (Price, 2001).

Action research provides a process through which teachers can systematically examine how what they do impacts student learning (Mills, 2007). In an era of accountability, preparation in action research provides teachers with an approach to inquiry that acknowledges their impact on student learning outcomes (Hendricks, 2009) while supporting them to explore alternative instructional strategies (Schoen, 2007) in an effort to continuously improve outcomes for children.

According to Schoen (2007), learning to conduct action research is a developmental process involving an acquisition phase, a fluency phase, and a generalization phase. In the acquisition phase, teachers or teacher candidates learn the skills of observation, goal identification, literature review, and data collection. These skills are then applied in the fluency phase, which includes instruction and collaboration. In the generalization phase, teachers are able to apply their ability to engage in action research methodology to novel situations without support. Schoen also identifies dispositional characteristics that may support success in action research: positive experiences with action, positive feelings about change, reflection and communication about pedagogical approaches, and psychological flexibility.

Teacher candidates may be limited in the type of action research they conduct during their student teaching placement. Student teachers search for the roles they might play within a borrowed classroom (Oyler et al., 2006). They may have little power to make changes in the school and may even be limited in making sustainable changes within a single classroom. Their focus is on survival within an environment over which they have very limited control. The student teacher may experience the following challenges to conducting action research: a limited number of takeover weeks (thus limiting the potential for multiple cycles of action), difficulty in balancing day-to-day teaching responsibilities while conducting action research, reduced decision-making power, and even cooperating teachers who may not support or value classroom action research. Cain, Holmes, Larrett, and Mattock (2007) suggest that in many cases, teacher candidates will engage in classroom action research that is literature-informed and involving a single cycle of action. Strong collaboration between the research course instructor, field instructor, and cooperating teacher can support the teacher candidate to move beyond a single cycle of action in response to student learning.

Action research reflects three dimensions or levels of concern: personal, professional, and political (Noffke, 1997). In their study of action research performed by teacher candidates, Cain et al. (2007) found that all three dimensions were addressed, but greatest emphasis was placed on the personal dimension. Specifically, teacher candidates were focused primarily on personal growth and self-awareness. While this may be developmental, contextual constraints may have limited the candidates' opportunities to address the professional dimension (increasing knowledge about teaching) and the political dimension (addressing issues of social justice).

Teacher candidates can be prepared to perform action research that recognizes the social contexts of schools. Zeichner and Gore (1995) describe how teacher candidates at the University of Wisconsin–Madison learned to think about educational problems and dilemmas beyond the personal level to examine the larger social contexts and implicit issues of social justice (the political dimension). Zeichner and Gore believe that all action research studies have the potential to address moral and political questions. Although teacher candidates might tend to frame a problem in a personal way, they can be supported to frame it within a larger context. For example, when considering the differences between her instructional approach and the cooperating teacher's approach, the teacher candidate can personalize the problem, or she may instead consider this problem within the larger framework of differential power within schools. University teacher preparation programs may support such development by providing examples of studies from previous teacher candidates that extend beyond the personal level and by illustrating how different frameworks can be applied to a single teaching dilemma.

Wansart (1995) asserts that special educators should be prepared to engage in action research that adheres to the following principles: (1) focus on abilities, (2) focus on advocacy, and (3) focus on improving teaching and the students' lives. A focus on abilities can be emphasized across multiple courses. For example, when engaging in the process of assessment, students can be expected to identify and write about relative student strengths as well as areas of need. Pedagogical courses can provide examples of how to consider learner strengths when selecting instructional approaches and strategies. Teacher candidates need support to identify different forms of advocacy and the types of advocacy they might engage in at different points in their career. Advocacy includes educating others (including children without disabilities) about the abilities, interests, and needs of children with disabilities. It also includes teaching children with disabilities to develop self-advocacy skills. Across their professional life span, special educators advocate for their "students as learners against the official institutional definitions of those who are unsuccessful in school, that is, underachiever, learning disabled, remedial, substandard" (Wansart, p. 171). Special educators support their colleagues in general education to include children with disabilities. This role as an inclusion facilitator may extend to improving students' lives by working toward greater participation in the community beyond the school.

Constructing knowledge through action research is not enough. Teachers need a way to display and share their knowledge with peers. Preservice teachers might accomplish this by sharing their work in poster sessions with peers or during faculty meetings at the practicum site

(Burnaford, 2001). Some programs share candidate work through publications, and still others include an oral presentation component (see the discussion below on Boston College's Community of Learners event).

General education teacher candidates may also be encouraged to engage in action research studies that include children with disabilities. Oyler et al. (2006) describe such a preservice teaching effort at Teachers College, Columbia University. This master's in education program offers a preservice inclusion study group that emphasizes teacher reflection and inquiry, with three major projects required: (1) a contextualized inquiry about one child that encourages teacher candidates to reexamine assumptions based on careful observation, (2) an examination of the existing published research on a question of interest, and (3) a school inquiry project that examines the school environment, communication between adults within the school and the community, and decision making. Students also complete two semesters of full-time student teaching. Oyler et al. present samples of teacher candidates' writings about their inclusive teaching experiences. Leslie Gore, one of the teacher candidates in the project, describes the relationship between the literature she studied and her day-to-day teaching:

> I did not always start off deciding to try something out that I agreed with or found interesting from the literature that I read. Often, it was in trying to make sense of what I was or was not doing that I went back to the research, reconciling my own experiences with this literature on inclusive education. In doing this, I was able to change my practice, to give certain practices a name, and in general, to maintain a high level of consciousness and deliberateness about the choices I was making and the ways I was thinking. (p. 80)

In addition to engaging general education teacher candidates in action research that addresses the needs of all learners, including children with disabilities, general and special education teacher candidates can be encouraged to engage in collaborative action research with one another. This may occur in the context of co-teaching opportunities. Preservice programs offer an ideal setting in which to instill values of collaboration between general and special educators. Examples of co-teaching and collaborative action research between general and special educators can be found in Chapter 2.

The increased focus on action research in preservice preparation is driven by the knowledge that engaging in action research is a form of professional development that can sustain a teacher across the professional life span. "Our premise is that to create better schools, teachers must be viewed in dramatically new ways: as leaders, researchers, and authors of their professional development" (Tafel & Fischer, 2001, p. 221).

ACTION RESEARCH IN TWO MASTER'S DEGREE PROGRAMS

Elements of the action research component of two special education teacher preparation programs are shared in this section. The discussion of Boston College's program emphasizes the philosophical foundations and institutional structures undergirding the action research component, whereas the discussion about the University of Central Florida's program emphasizes the evaluation of action research studies in special education.

Boston College

Boston College's programs in teacher education (including the programs in Moderate Special Needs and Severe Disabilities) are founded on five themes developed by the faculty in the Department of Teacher Education, Special Education, Curriculum & Instruction. These themes provide a foundation for all coursework (within the various department programs) and are reflected in the requirements of the final action research project. The five themes are (Teacher Education/Special Education, 2008):

- Promoting social justice: We see teaching as an activity with political dimensions and we see educators as responsible for challenging inequities in the social order and working with others to establish a more just society.
- Constructing knowledge: We regard all teachers and students as active agents in their own learning, who draw on prior knowledge and experience to construct new knowledge in interaction with texts, materials, and other learners.
- Inquiring into practice: The curriculum is intended to bridge the gap between research and practice by fostering critical reflection and by treating classrooms and schools as sites for teacher research and other forms of practitioner inquiry.
- Meeting the needs of diverse learners: We believe that one of the central challenges of teaching is meeting the needs of all learners, especially as the school population becomes more diverse in race, culture, ethnicity, language background and ability/disability.
- Collaborating with others: Prospective teachers are encouraged to collaborate with each of the stakeholders in the educational process (other teachers, administrators, human service professionals, parents, community members) and with fellow students and professors.

Throughout the programs, course syllabi, course orientations, course curricula, and assignments are structured to address these five themes, with the theme of social justice being central to program faculty efforts.

Social justice is interpreted by the faculty as being efforts to improve life chances for children.

As part of the programs' emphases on reflection, inquiry, and social justice, all students enrolled in department programs leading to teaching license eligibility must successfully complete two inquiry courses. The first inquiry course (one credit) is taken simultaneously with a one day per week pre-practicum. Key assignments include autobiography of learning (to support the identification of assumptions and biases and the role of lived experiences on teacher formation), formation of research questions, and a literature review. The second inquiry course (two credits) is taken simultaneously with the full practicum (five days per week student teaching experience). Students complete two critical reflection papers and an action research project paper that serves as the comprehensive examination. All action research studies must address pupil learning (which is construed broadly to include behavior and communication development) and teacher candidate learning outcomes.

The *Inquiry Project Handbook* (Department of Teacher Education, Special Education, Curriculum & Instruction, Boston College, 2008) reminds teacher candidates to reflect and act on the five department themes and the following four categories of inquiry when conducting their research and when writing their final inquiry project paper: (1) teacher as researcher, (2) content and pedagogy, (3) pupil learning, and (4) social justice. A rubric is used to score students' papers across these four areas of inquiry. Teacher candidates, faculty, cooperating teachers, and the practicum office staff attend a Community of Learners event that offers teacher candidates an opportunity to discuss their action research studies in a roundtable discussion format.

University of Central Florida

The University of Central Florida offers a Master of Education (M.Ed.) Program in Exceptional Education and a Masters of Arts (M.A.) in Exceptional Education. These programs place emphasis on the preparation of reflective practitioners who engage in inquiry. An action research project is required in both programs, although the requirements vary slightly. The action research project at the University of Central Florida is closely aligned with the College of Education's mission, which reads:

> The mission of the College of Education is to provide a high-quality education for its undergraduate students, graduate students and others as reflective practitioners, to promote and conduct research and scholarship, and to participate in learning communities that enhance practice and student outcomes.

Table 4.1. Action Research Project Rubric

Components	Exceeds Criteria	Meets Criteria	Below Criteria
Step One: Identifying and Investigating a Classroom Problem			
Literature Review	Eight or more sources clearly linked to this research are included. Sources are from peer-reviewed journals and are cited and referenced APA style. (18–20 pts.)	Five to seven sources linked to this research are included. Most sources are from peer-reviewed journals and are cited APA style with minor errors. (14–17 pts.)	Four or less sources are provided. Most sources are not from peer-reviewed journals. There are APA errors in citations and references. (13 or less pts.)
Purpose of the Study	Need/problem is clearly identified, supported with data, and clearly linked to research literature. A very clear explanation of the rationale and support for use of the intervention is provided. Specific research question is identified. (9–10 pts.)	Need/problem is identified, somewhat supported with data, and linked to research literature. Some explanation of the rationale and support for use of the intervention is provided. Research question is identified. (7–8 pts.)	Need/problem is unclear and is not supported with data. Explanation of the rationale and support for use of the intervention is lacking. A research question is not identified or is not clear. (6 or less pts.)
Step Two: Developing and Implementing an Action Research Plan			
Method	Comprehensive information is provided. Setting and participants are clearly described. Procedures, timelines, materials, and type of data collection are fully described (can easily be replicated with what is provided). (18–20 pts.)	Important information is provided. Setting and participants are described. Procedures, timelines, materials, and type of data collection are described (can be replicated, but not all tools and information are provided). (14–17 pts.)	Information is limited. Setting and participants are not clearly described. Procedures, timelines, materials, and type of data collection are unclear (difficult to replicate as written). (13 or less pts.)

Step Three: Collecting and Analyzing Data		
Results	Research steps are clearly pinpointed, including any modifications to the procedures. Actual collected data are included and are accurately labeled, scored, and dated. Well-formatted, comprehensive data display is provided (i.e., graph, table, chart, etc.). Narrative summarizes results and highlights salient features of collected data and data display. (18–20 pts.)	References to research steps are included. Some actual collected data are included. The majority of the data are clearly labeled, scored, and dated. Data display is provided (i.e., graph, table, chart, etc.). A narrative summary of the results is provided. (14–17 pts.)	Minimal references to research steps are included. Collected data are insufficient to answering the research question. Data are not clearly labeled or scored. Data are not summarized and no data display is presented. Narrative is limited and does not provide a summary of the results. (13 or less pts.)
Step Four: Using and Sharing the Results		
Discussion	Comprehensive summary of evidence is provided. Implications and limitations of the research are fully discussed, as well as recommendations for future study. Outcomes are clearly and specifically linked to professional literature. Clearly presented evidence shows growth as a teacher through this project. (18–20 pts.)	Summary of evidence is provided. Some implications and limitations of the research are discussed. Professional literature is mentioned, but is not clearly linked. Some evidence is included to show growth as a teacher through this project. (14–17 pts.)	Summary of the evidence is limited. Discussion does not include implications and limitations of the research or recommendations for future study. Link to professional literature not established. Discussion of professional growth is limited. (13 or less pts.)
Written Presentation	Writing flows with APA style and is organized with appropriate headings. Manuscript is portfolio ready, suitable for submission for publication. (9–10 pts.)	Manuscript has a few errors in grammar, punctuation, or spelling. Some headings are used. Manuscript is portfolio ready. (7–8 pts.)	Manuscript has many errors in grammar, punctuation, or spelling. It is not organized with headings. Manuscript is not portfolio-ready. (6 or less pts.)
TOTAL 100		

Adapted by C. E. Pearl (2008) from K. J. Miller (2000), *Evaluation Instrument for Action Research Project*.
*Action Research Steps adopted from *Improving Student Learning through Classroom Action Research*, Florida Department of Education, Bureau of Exceptional Education and Student Services (2004).

While faculty use similar rubrics in both programs, the rubric presented in Table 4.1 was adapted from a rubric created by Miller (2000) and is used with M.Ed. candidates enrolled in a federally funded (Office of Special Education Programs) project entitled Preparing Teachers to Work with Students with Autism Spectrum Disorders (Cynthia Pearl, co-principal investigator). The action research project aligns with the four major components of the action research process as articulated in a document developed by the Florida Department of Education, Bureau of Exceptional Education (2004) (see Table 4.1): (1) identifying a classroom problem, (2) developing an action research plan, (3) collecting and analyzing data, and (4) using and sharing results. These components are addressed in the preceding rubric, which is used to critique teacher candidate performance on the action research project.

The performance of an action research study is just one component within a larger teacher preparation effort focused on preparing the reflective practitioner. Teacher excellence and teacher retention may be supported through the preparation of reflective practitioners who have developed an inquiry stance. More importantly, children benefit from being served by teachers who engage in active reflection. Preservice preparation on action research provides teachers with a form of professional development that can sustain them across their professional life span. Schools play a critical role in supporting teachers to continue to develop as action researchers engaged in considering the personal, professional, and political dimensions of teaching.

REFERENCES

Burnaford, G. (2001). School and university teacher action research: Maintaining the personal in the public context. In G. Burnaford, J. Fischer, & D. Hobson (Eds.), *Teachers doing research* (2nd ed.)(pp. 193–219). Second edition. Mahwah, NJ: Erlbaum.

Cain, T., Holmes, M., Larrett, A., & Mattock, J. (2007). Literature-informed, one-turn action research: Three cases and a commentary. *British Educational Research Journal, 33*(1), 91–106.

Cochran-Smith, M., & Lytle, S. L. (2009). *Inquiry as stance: Practitioner research for the next generation.* New York: Teachers College Press.

Collins, B. C., Grisham-Brown, J., & Schuster, J. W. (1998). Training rural teachers as researchers: Guidelines for conducting field-based research in the rural classroom. In *Coming together: Preparing for rural special education in the 21st century.* Conference proceedings of the American Council on Rural Special Education, Charleston, SC, March 25–28, 1998. ED 417 909.

Cooper, J. M. (Series Editor) & Larrivee, B. (2006). *An educator's guide to teacher reflection*. Boston: Houghton.

Department of Teacher Education, Special Education, Curriculum & Instruction, Boston College (2008). *Inquiry project handbook*. Chestnut Hill, MA: Boston College.

Dewey, J. (1916). *Democracy and education*. New York: MacMillan.

Florida Department of Education, Bureau of Exceptional Education and Student Services. (2004). *Improving student learning through classroom action research: A guide to becoming an action researcher*. Tallahassee, FL: Author.

Griffith, A. S. (2005). Packing parachutes for the jump into education. *Teacher Education and Practice, 18*(3), 282–296.

Hendricks, C. (2009). Improving schools through action research: A comprehensive guide for educators (2nd ed.). Upper Saddle River, NJ: Pearson.

Hiebert, J., Morris, A. K., Berk, D., & Jansen, A. (2007). Preparing teachers to learn from teaching. *Journal of Teacher Education, 58*(1), 47–61.

Hobson, D. (2001). Action and reflection: Narrative and journaling in teacher research. In G. Burnaford, J. Fischer, & D. Hobson (Eds), *Teachers doing research* (2nd ed.)(pp. 7–27). Mahwah, NJ: Erlbaum.

Hobson, D., & Smolin, L. (2001). Teacher researchers go online. In G. Burnaford, J. Fischer, & D. Hobson (Eds.), *Teachers doing research.* (2nd ed.)(pp. 83–120). Mahwah, NJ: Erlbaum.

Malone, L. D., & Tulbert, B. L. (1996). Beyond content and pedagogy: Prepared centered teachers. *Contemporary Education, 68*(1), 45–48.

Miller, K. J. (2000). *Evaluation instrument for action research project*. Orlando: University of Central Florida.

Mills, G. E. (2007). *Action research: A guide for the teacher researcher.* (3rd ed.). Upper Saddle River, NJ: Pearson.

Noffke, S. E. (1997). Professional, personal, and political dimensions of action research. *Review of Research in Education, 22*(1), 305–343.

Oyler, C., and the preservice inclusion study group: Allaf, C., Hamre, B., Howard, S., Gore, L., Lee, J., & Wang, B. (2006). *Learning to teach inclusively: Student teachers' classroom inquiries*. Mahwah, NJ: Erlbaum.

Pedro, J. (2006). Taking reflection into the real world of teaching. *Kappa Delta Pi Record, 42*(3), 129–132.

Pine, G. J. (2009). Teacher action research: Building knowledge democracies. Los Angeles: Sage.

Price, J. (2001). Action research, pedagogy, and change: The transformation potential of action research in pre-service teacher education. *Journal of Curriculum Studies, 33*(1), 43–74.

Raisch, M. L. (1994). *Collaborative teacher research: Cooperating teacher, student teacher, and university faculty working together.* Paper presented at the Annual Meeting of the American Educational Research Association, New Orleans, LA, April 4–8. ED 372 087

Rose, R., & Grosvenor, I. (2001). Action research. In R. Rose & I. Grosvenor (Eds.), *Doing research in special education* (pp. 13–17). London: David Fulton Publishers.

Schoen, S. (2007). Action research: A developmental model of professional social-
    ization. *Clearing House: A Journal of Educational Strategies, Issues and Ideas, 80*(5),
    211–216.
Tafel, L. S., & Fischer, J. C. (2001). Teacher action research and professional devel-
    opment: Foundations for educational renewal. In G. Burnaford, J. Fischer, &
    D. Hobson (eds), *Teachers doing research* (2nd ed.)(pp. 221–235). Mahwah, NJ:
    Erlbaum.
Teacher Education/Special Education, Curriculum & Instruction. (2008). Retrieved
    January 5, 2010, from www.bc.edu/schools/lsoe/academics/departments/
    teseci.htm
Wansart, W. L. (1995). Teaching as a way of knowing: observing and responding
    to students' abilities. *Remedial and Special Education, 16*(3), 166–177.
Zeichner, K. M., & Gore, J. M. (1995). Using action research as a vehicle for stu-
    dent teacher reflection. In S. E. Noffke & R. B. Stevenson (Eds.), *Educational
    action research: Becoming practically critical* (pp. 13–30). New York: Teachers
    College Press.

PART II

THE GRADUATE STUDENT ACTION RESEARCH STUDIES

Chapters 5 through 8 are about action research studies conducted by master's degree students in general education (Catalano) and special education (Morillo, Spence, and Faletra) at Boston College. These were submitted in fulfillment of the comprehensive examination requirement for master's degree programs leading to eligibility for a teaching license in the state of Massachusetts. These studies were developed in response to authentic teacher concerns about the academic and linguistic performance or behavioral challenges of children with mild to severe disabilities. The papers featured in Chapters 5 through 8 were selected for their quality (each earned a grade of "distinction") and because collectively they address a diverse range of topics, contexts, and students.

Department faculty collaboratively developed a structure for the papers about the action research studies. The following structure was provided as a guideline for paper headings and content: Conceptual and Theoretical Framework (importance of the research question and primary theories that ground the study); Review of the Literature; Description of Context and Frame of Reference (including reflective narrative about the influence of the teacher candidate's personal and educational history and how that history influences teaching decisions along with a description of the classroom, school, and community contexts); Intervention (addressing both the content area and pedagogy); Data Sources (evidence of pupil and teacher learning); Results, Analysis and Interpretation, Implications (with an emphasis on implications for the teacher candidate's future practice); References; and Appendices.

An abstract was also required, but deleted for this text due to potential redundancy with the preface and the introductions presented below. Each of the inquiry papers (described briefly below) exemplify characteristics of quality action research discussed in Chapter 3, such as teacher ownership of the question and reflection about both student and teacher learning.

In Chapter 5, Claudia Morillo presents her action research study on teaching sight word vocabulary. Claudia's study grew out of her interest in six children with disabilities who were included in her second grade classroom. The following research question guided her inquiry: How can I use a variety of instructional strategies to help a student recognize and read high-frequency sight words? Claudia directly taught the pre-primer list of Dolch words through flash cards, games, and guided reading sessions to "Mitch," a boy with learning disabilities. She used the Curriculum Based Measurement (CBM) approach to assess and monitor his progress. Mitch's sight-word reading and attitude were positively impacted by her intervention. Claudia learned the value of progress monitoring and its relationship to effective instruction. Claudia earned distinction for this study, which exemplifies strong assessment practices, her collaborative efforts with general and special educators and the family, and her devotion to improving outcomes for her student. Strong connections to the BC themes and the four categories of inquiry (discussed in Chapter 4) are evident in this study.

Melissa Spence's study (Chapter 6) addressed the expressive communication needs of a student with autism and high verbal skills. The following research question guided her inquiry: "What happens to Vinnie's expressive communication when I implement a communication game into his academic program?" Melissa developed a communication game that integrated the use of color to correspond to three target areas of instruction: pronouns, verb conjugation, and verb tense. This study earned distinction and was selected to appear in this book because of its rich description of teacher researcher and student contexts and the quality of the intervention. Further, Melissa's teaching philosophy that education should be individualized, enjoyable, motivating to the student, and collaborative is evident in her study. Melissa's study also connects to the BC themes and the four types of inquiry discussed in Chapter 4.

Julie Catalano's inquiry project (Chapter 7) was guided by the following research question: "How will the math performance of my struggling students change if I offer them tutoring in a small-group setting as well as individually?" Julie's inclusive classroom was in a large urban setting that had adopted the use of the TERC Mathematics program. Her action research study addressed the problem of poor math performance in four students with specific learning disabilities and/or emotional disabilities by providing individual and small group tutoring sessions and by developing a math resource folder for each student. Julie earned distinction for this study that integrated the instruction of basic math concepts with opportunities to engage in higher-level math thinking. Julie reflected deeply about the affective side of learning, examining her students' emotional responses to math more generally and to the pullout tutoring session model.

In Chapter 8, Jim Faletra presents his action research study that was guided by the following research question: "What happens when a behavior plan is implemented to stop a student's head-slapping?" Jim applied Functional Behavior Analysis (FBA) and Positive Behavior Support (PBS) to address the self-abusive behaviors of a secondary student with severe disabilities. This study, which earned distinction, addressed the Boston College program themes and the four categories of inquiry discussed in Chapter 4. Jim also provided a clear description about how his own educational history influenced his teaching philosophy. Jim's study is particularly noteworthy because he engaged in multiple cycles of action grounded in reflection about the impact of his actions on student performance.

5

Teaching "Mitch" to Recognize and Read High-Frequency Sight Words

Claudia Morillo

In the spring of 2006, I was student teaching in an elementary public school in Newberry (a pseudonym). My placement was in an integrated second-grade classroom. This model was designed in a way that children with special needs were placed in a general education classroom, where a general education teacher and a special educator worked together planning and developing instruction. In my first weeks of student teaching, I began to think about the possible research questions I could develop.

Instead of randomly selecting a topic, I decided to start by reading the Individualized Educational Plans (IEPs) of the six students who were integrated in this classroom. I discussed with the classroom teachers the students' IEP goals and the progress they had accomplished halfway through the school year. The special educator expressed her concerns regarding one particular student who was not making significant progress toward his IEP goals. She expressed her interest in having me work one-on-one to support him in the different academic areas affected by his disability.

As written in Mitch's IEP, his goals for English Language Arts focused on his ability to develop an understanding of the conventions of print, relationship of letters, and patterns of spelling. One of the benchmarks indicated for this goal was that he would recognize and read high-frequency sight words from a list, although which list was not specified in the IEP. Based on this particular goal and after conducting informal assessments for several weeks, I decided to pursue the following research question: *How can I use a variety of instructional strategies to help Mitch recognize and read high-frequency sight words?* I was excited with the selection of my research question because it implied an action that was directly related to both teaching and learning. The research question was meaningful for me because I hoped to help a struggling reader make significant progress in his reading skills. The inquiry would also give me the opportunity to improve my practice as a special educator by using and developing a variety of instructional strategies that I could apply not only with this particular student, but also with future students who have special needs, as well as the general education population.

LITERATURE REVIEW

Throughout the years, research has shown that children need opportunities to learn different reading skills. Many researchers agree that these skills should be focused on spoken language, phonological awareness, phonics, fluency, word recognition, and comprehension (Armbruster, Lehr, & Osborn, 2003). Struggling readers usually present difficulties in some of these areas. The research question I developed directly addressed word recognition. It also addressed fluency, as the intervention focused on the teaching of sight words.

Sight words are defined by Richek, Caldwell, Jennings, and Lerner (2002) as those words that are recognized immediately, without having to analyze them. Bos and Vaughn (2006) define sight words as words whose pronunciation and meaning students can automatically recognize. They explain that reading words by sight means accessing the words stored in the memory. It requires the ability to read the words as a whole, without sounding them out. When children have a good recognition of sight words their reading comprehension improves because they spend less time trying to decode. The learning of sight words is especially important because research has shown that 99% of the words in children's texts are sight words. Richek et al. (2002) also suggest that children need help to develop this sight word vocabulary. Bos and Vaughn (2006) agree with this statement, as they wrote, "Regardless of their letter-sound predictability, words need to be taught so that they are automatically recognized" (p. 135). In a report from the National Reading Panel, a group of reading teachers, parents, educational administrators, and scientists found that when students receive guidance in reading, their fluency also improves (National Institute for Literacy, 2000).

Different lists of high-frequency sight words have been developed to guide teachers on the words that children will usually encounter when reading their books. A type of book frequently used for teaching sight words is pattern books. These books contain refrains that are repeated throughout the text, which foster and support word recognition (Richek et al., 2002). There are different popular series books that might be used with this purpose of teaching sight words, such as *The Sunshine Books* series, *The Story Box,* and *Traditional Tales,* among others. One problem that might be encountered with pattern books is that the student might memorize the text. As Richek et al. (2002, p. 177) state:

> Students with reading problems can best learn to recognize words by reading them in context. However, they may also need additional practice with words in isolation to reinforce automaticity and give them a sense of progress. Practicing individual words is useful for readers at many different levels. A core of sight words enables beginning readers to read easy books and serves as a basis for learning phonics.

Cunningham (2000) also suggests different guidelines that can be used when teaching sight words. He recommends that we provide multiple opportunities for the student to read the words in context and that the words be introduced before encountering them in a text. Guidelines from the guided reading approach may serve as a good way of helping students make these connections between the sight words and their meaning. Guided reading is a literacy approach in which particular texts at the child's reading level are selected for the students to read while the teacher monitors their reading behavior. Throughout the session the teachers promote conversations about the text, then encourage students to make predictions and connections with their real lives. After reading the book, the teacher scaffolds the students' learning by helping them develop different reading skills such as comprehension, decoding, and phonemic awareness, using the words in the text (Antonacci, 2000).

Cunningham (2000) provides several other instructional strategies that may be considered when teaching sight words. He states that the number of words introduced in a lesson must be limited. He also indicated that the recognition of words should be reinforced by adding a kinesthetic component such as tracing or writing the words. He also suggests that words that have been taught should be reviewed and that games can be used to promote quick word recognition.

WHO AM I AS A RESEARCHER?

Throughout these past years I have become aware of the large number of students with special needs who face difficulties in reading and comprehension. As a special educator, I was motivated to find effective ways to teach these struggling readers and help them make progress. In this research project, I was interested in making the silent reading period more meaningful for Mitch by using texts to teach him the sight words that came up. I believed that if Mitch increased his knowledge of high-frequency sight words, he would begin to enjoy reading silently. In the different courses I have taken, I have learned that when students spend less time trying to decode, they have more comprehension of the books they read.

I began the research with the belief that it would help me better understand the importance of teacher research and the impact it has on student learning. Having the opportunity to administer formal and informal assessments, to develop an intervention plan, and to monitor progress are all strategies that enhance my professional growth as a special educator.

Researching this topic helped me learn many teaching strategies that I will continue to put into practice in my future role as a special educator. This research question also helped me understand ways to modify the curriculum as I worked with a student with learning disabilities who was reading two levels below his grade level.

Throughout the research I was able to apply the Boston College themes by collaborating with the special educator in the classroom, who gave me feedback as I implemented the intervention techniques. I promoted social justice and accommodated diversity by working with a diverse population, giving a child with disabilities the same rights and opportunities for learning as his peers. I also constructed knowledge as I researched assessment methods and useful techniques to help students read. By investigating the current research on teaching children to read and implementing the techniques found, I applied the theme of taking inquiry into practice.

The school where this research took place was an elementary school, grades K–5, that has an enrollment of approximately 400 students. 84% of the student population is white, 7% Asian, 6% black, and 3% Hispanic. The school's vision statement focuses on building a community where teachers and students work together. Intellectual and social development is encouraged through a diverse curriculum. The school also emphasizes the importance of teaching children to explore and apply problem-solving strategies, to learn how to improve when they make mistakes, to respect and value all people, and to approach social and educational challenges with confidence and a positive attitude.

In these past months student teaching at this school, I have perceived their commitment to the education of each of their students. Teachers take into consideration the individual needs and make the necessary accommodations to help each student access learning. I have seen how everyone at the school supports one another. There is a great sense of collaboration among the teachers. I have also perceived parent involvement and integration. Collaboration is seen not only among the teachers but among the students as well. Classrooms seem to be safe environments where students are engaged in group work, hands-on activities, and active learning.

RESEARCH METHODOLOGY

Participant Description

Mitch is an 8-year-old boy who was born and raised in the United States. His primary language is English. He lives with his mother and his younger sister. He began school at the kindergarten level. During the past years, Mitch's family faced economic difficulties, which forced them to move several times. This has resulted in Mitch having to attend four different schools in the past four years.

Mitch is a very friendly and cooperative boy. He has a great relationship with his peers and is always willing to help them. He shows respect for his classroom teachers and follows the classroom rules. In the academic areas, Mitch has been struggling with reading and writing since kindergarten. For this reason, he was held back in kindergarten. Mitch's kindergarten teacher referred him to the special education team after noticing that he was making no progress even after 2 years of kindergarten. After an evaluation process, the multidisciplinary team determined that Mitch qualified for a Specific Learning Disability and that he displayed a lack of progress in the general education curriculum. Mitch was struggling and making little progress in several academic areas such as reading, writing, and math. The team decided that Mitch would benefit from being integrated into a general education classroom and developed an Individualized Educational Plan for him.

Based on the work of Burnaford, Fischer, and Hobson (2001), the research method used throughout this inquiry can be called teacher research. They suggest that teacher research involves having teachers research a particular question and develop an intervention with a desired outcome. This teacher research was a collaborative and systematic method that involved keeping journals, taking inventories, creating lesson plans, and collecting and analyzing student work. One important characteristic of this method is that it required ongoing reflection about practice.

In this teacher research project, mixed methods of data collection were used. Qualitative data collection took place through the observations and interviews that provided nonquantifiable data. Quantitative data collection was used because different assessments were given that provided quantifiable data about the number of sight words the student was learning.

Data Sources

In order to better plan the intervention, in the first few weeks, I used several informal assessment tools as data sources. I gathered useful information by reading about Mitch's current level of performance as well as the goals and objectives in his Individualized Educational Plan. These informal types of assessment were used to learn more about Mitch's interests, strengths, and weaknesses.

I began this research paper by conducting an observation during Mitch's silent reading time. During this period, children are expected to select "just-right books" to read silently and independently. Just-right books are texts that are at the child's reading level. As I observed Mitch for 10 minutes, I noted that during this time he looked over six different books. He did not make attempts to read the words in the text; instead, he focused only on the pictures.

The home–school relationship and communication were important in supporting student learning. I had the opportunity to be present during the report card conference with Mitch's mother. During this meeting she expressed her concerns about the slow progress of her son and wanted to know ways in which she could help him at home. In order to get information regarding Mitch's attitude toward reading, I administered the Garfield Reading Inventory. As indicated by his percentile rank of 26, Mitch's reading attitude was as high as or better than 26% of the students in his class. It was interesting to see that he had a more positive attitude toward academic reading in contrast to recreational reading. Important information that I got from this survey is that he liked reading in school and starting a new book, but he didn't like the silent reading time or reading out loud. This inventory was given at the beginning and at the end of the intervention plan with the purpose of seeing how his attitude toward reading changed with the intervention.

An informal reading inventory was also administered to determine Mitch's reading levels, his independent, instructional, and frustration level. This information helped me select a list of just-right books to use during his silent reading time. The books selected contained the high-frequency words to be taught. A type of book helpful with the teaching of sight words was the pattern books. These books contained refrains that were repeated throughout the text, which fostered and supported word recognition (Richek et al., 2002).

As another valuable data resource, I interviewed the special educator in Mitch's classroom. She provided me with the list of Dolch Sight Words (see www.dolchsightwords.com) that children at the second-grade level are expected to master. I then decided to give Mitch a sight word assessment in order to determine which words he already knew and where to begin the intervention. He was asked to orally read the words in the pre-primer list presented in flash cards. Mitch was able to read 20 of 40 words. This assessment was administered again the following week, when he was able to read 18 of 40 words. This information served as a baseline to begin the intervention.

The *Informal Reading-Thinking Inventory* (Manzo, Manzo, & Mckenna, 1995) was also administered. After administering the pre-primer word list, it was evident that the intervention had to begin with the pre-primer sight word list, since he had 7 errors out of 15 words.

Monitoring Mitch's progress and growth throughout the intervention was a vital part of this research. Journals, anecdotal notes, and systems to mark and register the words that he was acquiring (including the ones that need further teaching and review) were all helpful tools. The results of the assessments previously mentioned will be described in detail in the "Results" section of this paper.

Description of the Intervention

The assessment procedures previously described helped in the intervention decisions. By knowing Mitch's reading level, I was able to set the goal for the intervention: Mitch would be able to orally read the complete pre-primer list of sight words with 90% accuracy by the end of the school year.

The intervention consisted of one-on-one sessions where different strategies were implemented. Three times a week, I sat with him during his silent reading time for a period of 40 minutes. The purpose of the lessons was to teach one or two new sight words in both isolation and context, then to review words presented in previous lessons. To introduce the words, I integrated a multisensory approach to teach the sight words. I started the lessons by applying steps from the *Sight Word Association Procedure* (SWAP) described by Bos and Vaughn (2006). First, I showed the words on cards and discussed their meaning with Mitch. I then read the words to him, shuffled them, and asked him to identify them. After he had heard and read the words, he would then trace the word with his fingers using different materials such as paper, sand, and a lacing pad.

In order to integrate the words in context, I applied strategies suggested by the *Guided Reading* approach. For each session I selected beginning reading level books that contained the same sight words introduced in isolation. Most of the books used were from the *Scholastic* collection's *High-Frequency Reader*, and from *Reading A–Z: The Online Guided Reading Program* (2006)(see www.readinga-z.com). Before the reading, Mitch was asked to talk about the cover of the book and make predictions. He first read the book silently and then out loud. Mitch was also asked to identify the sight words as they came up in the book by drawing a circle around them.

Following the reading, we often engaged in activities to provide Mitch practice in recognizing the sight words, as well as basic vocabulary and key concepts from the books. Some activities and games suggested by Novelli (2002) were used, such as having him connect letters written on index cards to make words, bingo games using the words, and matching pictures to words. Other activities used to reinforce his learning of the sight words were:

- Filling in the missing letters.
- Completing a paragraph using the words in the word bank.
- Using the sight words to describe the pictures shown.
- Unscrambling sight words.
- Drawing a line from the word to the correct picture.
- Playing sight word bingo with a peer.
- Finding rhyming words.

As part of the intervention, Mitch had a "Words I Know" book. Every week, he chose the words he was able to read automatically and pasted them in his "Words I Know" book. Under each word, he wrote a sentence using it. Another important part of the intervention was extending the goal into the home. In collaboration with Mitch's mother, each week he took home a list of the sight words introduced that week. As part of his homework, he had to read the words every night to his mother and bring back to school a record sheet of every time he read.

In order to assess and document Mitch's learning, the Curriculum Based Measurement (CBM) model was used. Curriculum Based Measurement is a method of monitoring student educational progress through direct assessment of knowledge and skills taught in a selected curriculum. Informal inventories, running records, rubrics, and checklists are all CBM techniques. In order to collect continuous assessment on Mitch's progress each week, an informal sight word assessment was given that asked him to orally read the complete pre-primer list of sight words. His number of correct words read was recorded and later graphed. Running records were also used. Through the running record, Mitch's reading aloud performance was recorded, making note of the number of correct words read, number of errors, and total words read per minute. This showed Mitch's progress throughout the intervention, as well as his accuracy rate.

RESULTS

Reading Sight Words from a List

The intervention phase on this inquiry project lasted 9 weeks. During this time I was able to keep a record of Mitch's progress. The weekly record sheet used throughout this time showed that Mitch increased his recognition and ability to automatically read aloud the pre-primer Dolch list of sight words when presented using flash cards (see Figure 5.1).

The first 2 weeks were devoted to baseline data collection. During the baseline period, Mitch automatically read an average of 18 of 40 words. After the intervention and use of the different instructional strategies, Mitch increased his ability to automatically read words to 37 of 40 words. This shows that he learned to automatically recognize and read from flash cards an average of two or three new words per week.

Reading Accuracy

Reading A–Z: The Online Reading Program (2006) defines the following accuracy rate levels: easy enough for independent reading (95–100% accuracy), instructional level for use in guided reading (90–94% accuracy), too difficult, will frustrate the reader (89% and below accuracy). As indicated by the first running record given and the informal reading test, Mitch began the intervention at an aa reading level with an accuracy of 88%. The running records used throughout the intervention to assess Mitch's reading performance as he read from a book showed that

Figure 5.1. Dolch Pre-Primer List Assessment Progress Monitoring

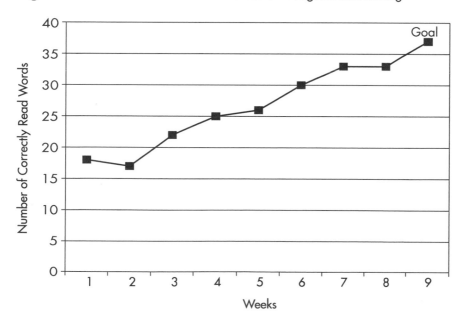

his accuracy rate improved. His reading accuracy changed throughout the intervention as he progressed to Level A books, being able to show a 90% accuracy rate by the end of the intervention. Level B books remained too difficult for him (at 63% accuracy).

Reading Attitude

Mitch's reading attitude was measured at the beginning and the end of the intervention using the *Elementary Reading Attitude Survey*, also known as the *Garfield Reading Survey* (McKenna & Kear, 1990). His recreational reading attitude went from the 25th percentile pre-intervention to the 62nd percentile post-intervention, meaning that his attitude is the same as or higher than the attitude of 62% of students when compared to the norms of his age. His academic reading attitude was higher than his recreational attitude toward reading. He began with a percentile rank of 32, which increased to the 78th percentile, indicating that his attitude toward academic reading is the same as or higher than the attitude of 78% of all students when compared to the norms of his age. In full scale his reading attitude went from the 26th percentile at the start of the intervention to a reading attitude in the 71st percentile after the intervention.

Constructing Meaning

The observations done during Mitch's silent reading time also revealed a change in the way he approached books. In the observation of the first weeks during the silent reading time, Mitch seemed to focus his attention only on the pictures of the book and quickly changed from book to book. In the following weeks he selected books that had been used during the intervention. He began to focus on particular books, showing interest in the text by pointing to each of the words as he read them silently.

As seen in the anecdotal notes, M was able to complete most of the activities done throughout the intervention, but required help. He especially requested assistance to read the instructions in the worksheets. Throughout the intervention M added new words to his "Words I Know" book. As he made sentences with the sight words, he showed good understanding of the meaning of the words, constructing logical sentences. When writing the words in a sentence he also requested assistance and depended on the flash cards to copy the sight words.

During the guided reading Mitch made logical predictions about the text based on the context clues. When responding to questions about the story he demonstrated good listening and reading comprehension. Each of the texts selected for the administration of the running records contained sight words that had been introduced in previous weeks. When reading these sight words in context, Mitch was able to automatically read 80% of the sight words.

DISCUSSION

From the beginning of the intervention, Mitch showed a positive attitude toward the individualized lessons. His sense of cooperation and willingness to work one-on-one during his silent reading time had a great impact on the process of the intervention. The use of games like bingo and the variety of activities such as fill in the blanks and matching seemed to engage and motivate Mitch.

Mitch's IEP served as a good frame of reference, giving me a better knowledge of his strengths and weakness. But as I read the IEP, I noticed that many of the goals were not measurable. It was stated in his English Language Arts goal that he would read sight words from a list. The IEP should indicate which list of sight words M should be able to read and how. My cooperating teacher suggested that I start by teaching him the sight words from the Dolch list. As I reviewed the books at Mitch's reading level, I confirmed that the Dolch list was a good starting point because many of those words frequently came up in the books.

The use of pattern books was a key element for the intervention. The repetition found in all books fostered Mitch's recognition of the sight words. This frequent exposure to the words helped Mitch store the words in his memory, which is a key process in sight word recognition described by Bos and Vaughn (2006). It was evident that Mitch was storing the words in his memory because on several occasions when he saw a word he stated that he had seen that word, and after thinking for several seconds he remembered and automatically read it without decoding. I did feel that some of the pattern books were more appropriate for younger ages, since the main ideas were very simple. This limited my ability to work on comprehension skills with Mitch.

Cunningham's (2000) statement that sight words need to be taught both in isolation and in context was evident throughout the intervention. By presenting the words on flash cards and having him write them and spell them before the guided reading, he was able to recognize the words as they came up. At the same time, reading the words in the text helped him better understand their meaning. His understanding was shown as he constructed his own sentences using the introduced sight words.

Observing the other students in the class and reviewing the second grade frameworks showed me that Mitch was significantly behind his group; therefore, working one-on-one with him was a necessary and appropriate approach. Time issues were definitely a limitation of the intervention. The original plan of the intervention was to have the one-on-one sight word sessions three times a week. Unfortunately, Mitch was absent 5 days, which limited the intervention frequency to about two times a week. Reinforcement and frequent exposure to the words had an impact on Mitch's learning. The weekly sight words assessment demonstrated that during the weeks he was absent the total amount of words acquired was lower than weeks when he wasn't absent. Instead of planning three 30-minute lessons, I could have considered giving 15-minute mini-lessons every day. This constant exposure to the words would help him retain them (Bos & Vaughn, 2006).

Recent research states that homework has a positive effect on school achievement for students with moderate disabilities and serves as a way of extending home–school partnership (Turnbull & Turnbull, 2001). Unfortunately, besides the fact that at the beginning of the intervention Mitch's mother agreed to follow up at home with the classroom activities, her support was not shown throughout the intervention. During several weeks throughout the intervention Mitch failed to complete the weekly assignment of reading a group of sight words to an adult on a daily basis. Analyzing the weekly sight word assessment, as well as the anecdotal notes, I noticed a relationship between Mitch's achievement and his homework completion. Even though the group of words he took home were words that had already been introduced at school, when he failed to complete his homework he showed difficulties remembering and automatically identifying them. This shows that the lack of home–school partnership might be affecting Mitch's achievement in school.

The "Words I Know" book served as a self-monitoring resource for Mitch. Many times he counted to see how many words he had learned. He showed enthusiasm every time he pasted a new word into the book. This also happened with the weekly sight word assessment. In the early weeks of the intervention I did not share with Mitch the data gathered by the assessment. But as the weeks progressed, he became interested in tracking his learning. Each week we counted together to see if he had a higher total of words automatically read. When Mitch began to monitor his own learning he seemed to put more effort into learning new words. Through the running records I was able to see a relationship between word recognition and reading fluency. The records showed that Mitch's reading accuracy rate increased throughout the intervention.

Measuring attitude has always been a difficult task. The *Garfield Reading Survey*, an adaptation of the *Elementary Reading Attitude Survey* (McKenna & Kear, 1990), was a great resource. As Mitch was able to recognize more words in the texts, his enjoyment of reading increased. It was interesting to see that his attitude toward academic reading was higher than his attitude toward recreational reading. This difference might have been caused by the fact that he was required to do academic reading with one of the teachers. Mitch doesn't have this type of support or guidance with recreational reading.

CONCLUSION AND RECOMMENDATIONS

Throughout the intervention Mitch was able to show significant progress toward the recognition of sight words, which was the primary goal of this project. Working one-on-one with Mitch and using a variety of instructional strategies was an effective approach in helping Mitch to improve his reading skills. As a special educator and researcher in this project, I learned the value of teaching sight word recognition. The improvement in Mitch's reading accuracy and the changes in his reading attitude reveal the positive effects that sight word recognition has on the reading process.

From the beginning it was evident that Mitch needed individualized instruction. Through the intervention Mitch was able to master 92% of the pre-primer list of sight words. For the rest of the school year, continued instruction is needed on more advanced lists of sight words. I ask myself what would have happened to Mitch's reading performance if he had been explicitly taught high-frequency sight words since the beginning of the school year. What impact would that have had on his reading level? Would he currently be reading higher-leveled books? Mitch should continue to be exposed to the sight words both in isolation and in context in order to maintain the progress he is making in reading accuracy. Using a combination of teaching sight words in isolation and in context was an important component of this intervention. In order to maintain Mitch's progress, classroom teachers need to continue to foster a balanced reading approach that would expose him to reading and phonemic awareness.

In the course of this research I valued the use of progress monitoring. Taking anecdotal notes, making observations, and graphing Mitch's performance in weekly assessments served as guidelines throughout the intervention. By tracking Mitch's progress, I was able to monitor my own teaching strategies and was able to determine if the intervention was being effective or if a restructure was needed. Mitch's second grade classroom teachers need to develop and implement progress monitoring techniques not only for Mitch, but for the rest of the students as well. A paired reading program is also recommended for Mitch. Through this program, Mitch would have the opportunity to work in pairs with another student, reading together and supporting each other while reading. The goal of this intervention would be to increase Mitch's reading fluency, word recognition, and comprehension.

As a student whose learning disabilities are affecting his progress, Mitch needs to have an Individualized Educational Plan that states the areas affected by his disability and a clear description of his current level of performance, which includes his annual goals, necessary accommodations, and specially designed instruction. Mitch's current IEP was written by the IEP team in his previous school. This IEP should be revised and new measurable and obtainable goals should be created, especially since the current special educator said that she doesn't clearly understand some of the written goals.

Working so closely with Mitch for these past months has helped me to see him as a bright, caring, and enthusiastic boy whose school achievement has been greatly affected by his learning disabilities and family difficulties. Having the opportunity to work with Mitch was a learning experience and a demonstration of what my responsibilities as a special educator might look like in my near future. Through this research experience I realized that principals, general educators, and families rely on us as special educators to help those students who are having difficulties making progress and meeting the curriculum frameworks for their grade level. As stated by many of my college professors, the responsibility of teaching children with disabilities should be shared among all. In this particular research there was good collaboration among the teachers who frequently discussed Mitch's progress, but there was a lack of partnership between home and school. Communication and partnership between Mitch's mother and the classroom teachers needs to strengthen. Frequent phone calls, notes to the home, and informal meetings need to be held to share Mitch's progress and communicate new goals.

Ongoing in this research project was a positive learning experience. Teacher research redefines our role as teachers. I was able to value teacher research as a tool that empowers us to make changes in the educational process both in our own schools and classrooms. Through this particular research I was able not only to teach, but also to improve and make an impact on my teaching skills and on the learning process of a student.

REFERENCES

Antonacci, P. A. (2000). Reading in the zone of proximal development: Mediating literacy development in beginner readers through guided reading. *Reading Horizons, 41*(1), 19–33.

Armbruster, B., Lehr, F., & Osborn, J. (2003). *A child becomes a reader.* Portsmouth, NH: RMC Research Corporation.

Bos, C. S., & Vaughn, S. (2006). *Strategies for teaching students with learning and behavioral problems.* Boston: Allyn and Bacon.

Burnaford, G., Fischer, J., & Hobson, D. (2001). *Teachers doing research: The power of action through inquiry.* Mahwah, NJ: Erlbaum.

Cunningham, P. M. (2000). *Phonics they use: Words for reading and writing* (3rd ed.). New York: Longman.

Dolch Sight Words. Retrieved June 9, 2009, from http://www.dolchsightwords.org.

Manzo, A., Manzo, U., & Mckenna, M. (1995). *Informal reading-thinking inventory.* Belmont, CA: Thomson-Wadsworth.

McKenna, M. C., & Kear, D. J. (1990). Measuring attitude toward reading: A new tool for teachers. *The Reading Teacher, 43*(9), 626–639.

National Institute for Literacy. (2000). *Report of the national reading panel.* Washington, DC: National Reading Panel.

Novelli, J. (2002). *Sight word games.* New York: Scholastic.

Reading A–Z: The Online Guided Reading Program. (2006). Retrieved June 9, 2009, from http://www.readinga-z.com.

Richek, M. A., Caldwell, J. S., Jennings, J. H., & Lerner, J. W. (2002). *Reading problems: Assessment and teaching strategies.* Boston: Allyn and Bacon.

Turnbull, A., & Turnbull. R. (2001). *Families, professionals, and exceptionality.* Upper Saddle River, NJ: Merrill-Prentice Hall.

6

Using a Communication Game to Improve the Expressive Language Skills of a Boy with Autism

Melissa Spence

Communication takes many forms, both verbal and nonverbal, such as speaking, sign, gestures, and eye gaze. No matter the form, individuals utilize communication to transmit needs and wants as well as to interact with others. Effective communication skills are important in many aspects of life; however, these skills play a pivotal role in school. In the classroom, effective communication is imperative, as learning consists of series of interactions between the teacher and students, and "the success of these interactions . . . depends heavily on their ability to communicate effectively" (Downing, 1999, p. 7). Therefore, it is essential to foster the development of communication skills in the classroom, as such skills play a vital role in the learning process.

There are two types of communication: receptive and expressive. Receptive communication is the understanding of the intent of the message conveyed by other individuals. Expressive communication is the ability to express wants, needs, or additional intents to others. Communication skills consist of the behaviors, including words, used to either indicate understanding (receptive skills) or to convey thought (expressive skills) (Downing, 1999). Effective expressive language skills not only provide students an avenue through which to display their knowledge, but also allow teachers to evaluate their students' learning. However, this process is hindered when working with students with autism, as these students exhibit marked verbal communication impairments. Only about 50% of individuals with autism become verbal (Towbin, Mauk, & Batshaw, 2002), and those who are verbal often exhibit language deficits such as inabilities to initiate or sustain conversation with others, idiosyncratic language, or a failure to learn the rules guiding verbal language (American Psychiatric Association, 2000; Rutter, 1978).

In my classroom there is one student who displays many of these communication impairments. Vinnie is a 9-year-old boy diagnosed with autism. He has been in self-contained special education classrooms for the last 3 years; however, next year he will begin integration into a general education setting. Although Vinnie is verbal, he consistently makes expressive communication errors.

Vinnie's deficits in expressive communication are impeding my ability to evaluate his learning. For example, it is difficult to test Vinnie's reading comprehension. When retelling a story or answering questions about a story, it is difficult to assess whether his pronoun, tense, and conjugation errors stem from reading comprehension difficulties or whether they exist as a function of poor expressive communication. Additionally, it is difficult to assess Vinnie's vocabulary when he inserts incorrect pronouns into sentences. For example, Vinnie will say "Don't touch my Vinnie" if a peer hits him in the knee. Is this error a symptom of vocabulary weaknesses (i.e., not knowing the word "knee"), or is it a lack of knowledge about pronoun rules? I believe Vinnie's communication errors result from deficits in his expressive communication repertoire, as is typically displayed by students with autism, and not a lack of knowledge in a particular skill area (i.e., vocabulary). Therefore, I want to develop an intervention that addresses these underlying deficits and focuses on the communicative areas in which Vinnie needs improvement. Thus, my research question is: What happens to Vinnie's expressive communication when I implement a communication game into his academic program?

There are three reasons why I consider it imperative to improve Vinnie's expressive communication. First, improving Vinnie's communication skills will enhance his overall learning. Expressive skills provide a method for me, as Vinnie's teacher, to more accurately assess his learning and offer him a direct avenue to communicate his knowledge. Second, communication skills are essential in the development of friendships, as communication allows one to participate and interact with peers (Goldstein, 2002; Schnorr, 1997). Improving Vinnie's communication skills will increase his access to peers, thereby aiding in the development of friendships. This will be especially important next year, when Vinnie begins integration, as he will have the opportunity to create a social circle outside the special education classroom. Last, developing an intervention for Vinnie will aid the creation of communication interventions not only for current students, but for future students as well. I am honing my skills and knowledge in the field by going through the process of a communication intervention specially targeted toward the expressive communication skills of students with autism.

THEMATIC COMPONENTS

My question of inquiry incorporates all my students (both present and future) by addressing the themes inherent in my Boston College education. These themes include social justice, diversity, constructing knowledge, collaboration, and inquiry into practice. My question addresses social justice, as it implicitly states that all students are worth teaching. This thematic statement often materializes during discussions concerning lower-functioning students; however, my question addresses the opposite issue. Vinnie is one of the higher functioning students in the class. This fact should not preclude him from instruction to improve his communication skills. As a teacher, it can be easy to focus attention on those students who are in most need of developing their remedial skills; however, it is just as important to place instructional focus on all students, even those who seemingly need less intensive intervention. Similarly, the question addresses diversity by challenging me to meet the needs of all learners. As previously stated, my intervention will help me learn how to differentiate instruction for individual students, thus aiding in the development of future communication interventions.

The question allows me to construct new knowledge by drawing on my prior knowledge of and experience with autism and its related communication challenges. Furthermore, my previous experience with communication assessments will aid in conceiving and implementing a program to attend to Vinnie's communication deficits. The theme of collaboration is also addressed, as I will gather input from my cooperating teacher to help document Vinnie's progress before, during, and after the intervention. By inquiring into my practice, my teaching methods (i.e., assignments, assessments, etc.) are likely to change. Creating an individualized intervention that is not designed for all students leaves future programs open to individual student adaptation.

EDUCATIONAL EXPERIENCES
AND PHILOSOPHY

Picture a city with one main street, one safe central park filled with children playing, and a spacious public library filled to the brim with brightly illustrated children's books. This is the city where the first 18 years of my education occurred. Nestled between the Angeles National Forrest and the city of Los Angeles, this small Southern California city is the picturesque destination of numerous families, settling there in order to provide a safe living environment and quality education for their children.

For all of its idyllic features, the public schools are the most prized accomplishment of the city. Students continually score in the top 10% of California students, and the district has a reputation for having some of the best teachers and resources in the area. All campuses are clean, safe, and conducive to learning. There is never a lack of books or school supplies, and what parents cannot readily provide for their children is easily supplied by the community. Although the district spends less per pupil than the state average, organizations such as the Boosters, Friends of Drama, PTA/PTSA, and Music Parents have seemingly unlimited funds and resources to make sure that students in the community have access to the best possible education.

Vinnie's school environment is a direct contrast to the one in which I grew up. Situated in the heart of a large urban city, the school is truly a diverse community. The majority of the school's population includes African Americans and Hispanics, very representative of the surrounding community. There are many self-contained special education classrooms, but there are also several integrated classrooms. The school's Web site stresses the importance of parent participation, stating that the school works very closely with parents, as they are children's most important teacher. However, I have rarely seen parents at school and I have never seen a parent in my classroom. It is hard to generalize parental involvement from just the experiences in my own classroom, as we are rather self-contained, but I know the parents of my students work very hard and do not have time to participate in numerous school activities. This is most likely true for most families in the school.

Recollections about my elementary and junior high school years are filled with memories of fun and learning. During these years, I believed school to be an institution of knowledge, a place to provide students with necessary facts and skills for future learning. However, my elementary and middle schools had contrasting methods to accomplish these goals. The purpose of elementary school was to enrich young minds and to supply children with the building blocks of education through individualized instruction. I came to believe that learning was the product of hard, individual work. In contrast, my junior high school teachers relied more on fun activities and group learning. They had neither the time nor resources to provide individualized instruction. Through my educational experiences, I have adopted the position that learning should be individualized, fun, and collaborative, and it is my objective to bring this conviction to my intervention with Vinnie. As an intervention, I have designed a communication game. The game is fun to play, and collaborative efforts were utilized in its conception. Furthermore, the game's content is highly individualized to address Vinnie's educational needs.

LITERATURE REVIEW

There is a dearth of research in the field of expressive communication for older, verbal individuals with autism. Available research focuses on instructional strategies for communication in regard to students with autism; however, this body of literature tends to center on augmentative and alternative communication modalities for low to nonverbal students. A second body of literature focuses on early intervention, particularly between the ages of 2 and 4. As Vinnie is verbal and older, neither of these bodies of work pertains directly to his intervention needs. As a result, I focused on the research surrounding the best instructional practices for overall communication development.

In recent years, the focus on instruction of communication skills has shifted. Previously, skills were taught in a mass-trial, one-to-one format. Proponents argued that the teaching of communication skills is more effective when instruction is simplified by breaking down learning into small units of instruction (Erba, 2000; Smith, 2001). Utilizing this teaching technique exposes children to the complex language intricacies, while drilling children in each component ensures mastery of these skills. Recently, however, opponents of mass-trial teaching argue that this type of drilled instruction limits spontaneous language use and generalization of skills (Goetz & Sailor, 1988; Smith, 2001).

Today, there is a greater focus on the use of natural contexts for communication instruction. That is, the student's natural daily environment is utilized to promote communication so that ". . . communication partners in the environment facilitate communication expression and that specific procedures [are] developed and used to prompt and consequate communication use" (Westling & Fox, 2004, p. 277). Additionally, generalization of language skills is much higher when a naturalistic approach is utilized (Koegel, Camarata, Valdez-Menchaca, & Koegel, 1998). However, children with autism do not learn in the same way as their non-autistic peers. These children have difficulty learning from their environment via exploration, modeling, and communication (Smith, 2001). Therefore, the incidental learning proposed by the research will not be effective for teaching communication to students with autism.

Although children with autism exhibit difficulty with incidental learning, they do display a propensity for visual learning (Goldstein, 2002). Teaching communication skills will be more effective if the language stimulation is presented with a visual modality. Teaching in this fashion capitalizes on an area of relative strength for many children with autism.

I have developed a communication intervention for Vinnie based on the unique learning styles of students with autism. The intervention does not rely on incidental learning practices, but instead involves components broken down into smaller units of instruction. Additionally, the game is highly visual, containing colors, pictures, and written words, in order to capitalize on the documented visual strengths of children with autism.

INTERVENTION

My most salient goal as a special education teacher is not to "normalize" my students. Too often, I believe the goal of special education services is to mold individuals toward society's definition of "normal." Not everyone fits this mold. Students in all classrooms do not learn the same way, are not interested in the same subjects, and function at varying ability levels. Such differences predominate in special education classrooms. I aim to teach every student to the best of his or her abilities, not to the definition of what they "should" be. My intervention addresses this goal, as I aim to modify the curriculum in a way that not only addresses Vinnie's unique needs, but also does so in a manner that maximizes his learning potential (i.e., visual, mass-trial, one-to-one format, etc.). By presenting the intervention in a game format, it becomes a fun, social, and engaging activity and not a didactic lesson.

Pre-Intervention Assessment

Before designing the game, I conducted an informal expressive communication assessment. This assessment demonstrated that Vinnie possessed deficits in the following areas: verbs, adjectives, adverbs, nonsymbolic language, pronouns, expanded concepts, three-word relations, complex negation, verb tense, conjunctions, and complex questions. These results matched my own and my cooperating teacher's observations. I selected three areas to serve as the focus of my intervention: pronouns, verbs (specifically verb conjugation), and verb tense.

Apparatus

The game board was designed with colored squares forming a path from start to finish. Each colored space correlated to color-coded question cards. There were three colors on the game board and each pertained to a different skill area: pronoun usage, verb conjugation, and verb tense. For example, the yellow cards addressed pronoun usage, while the orange cards concentrated on verb conjugation. Each card contained a picture, a picture with a word, or just a word. Although the pronoun and verb conjugation question cards could be used to measure both domains, by concentrating on only one area, I was better able to collect specific data and instruct Vinnie on one skill at a time.

Pronouns

The pronoun cards had a picture of a boy, girl, or group of individuals engaging in an activity. When picked, Vinnie described the picture using one sentence (i.e., "The boy is reading a book"). Pronouns were also addressed between each player's turn. Before the die was rolled, I asked Vinnie, "Whose turn is it?" He then had the opportunity to use the correct pronoun in order to identify whose turn was next.

Verb Conjugation

The verb conjugation cards also contained an action picture, but the picture was accompanied by a written verb. Vinnie conjugated the verb in order to use it to describe the picture. For example, a card would have a picture of a boy chasing a dog with the word "chase" above the picture. The correct answer would be: "He is chasing the dog." In addition to the cards, there were four spaces on the game board giving a directive: *scratch your nose, clap your hands, make a silly face*, and *jump*. When Vinnie performed the action, I asked him what he was doing so he could conjugate the verb in order to answer the question.

Verb Tense

The verb tense cards consisted of nine verbs, each one in present (i.e., *plays*) or past (i.e., *played*) tense. Only past tense verbs ending in –*ed* were used. When picked, Vinnie identified the tense of the verb on the card.

Intervention Procedure

To play the game, a player rolled the die, moved forward the number of spaces rolled, and picked a card based on the colored space landed upon. The game contained no punishers. That is, no space directed a player to loose a turn or to move backward, and there were no consequences if Vinnie answered a question card incorrectly. He was simply prompted or the correct sentence was modeled for him. There were some fun spaces on the game board (i.e. "Move forward three spots"), so that the game did not become too monotonous. Vinnie's peers were invited to play with him;

however, I was always present to record data and ensure proper speech patterns so that Vinnie did not receive incorrect information. Concerned about satiation, I did not want Vinnie to play every day. The point of the game was for Vinnie to have repetitive exposure to correct language formation in order to improve his own language learning. Therefore, we played the game two to three times per week for 6 weeks.

At the conclusion of the 6 weeks, I conducted three post-intervention tests, one for each skill area. Similar to the baseline assessment, I randomly selected cards to test Vinnie. For pronouns and verb conjugation, I chose five cards. He gave me the answer verbally, I wrote it down, and he copied the sentence onto his own paper. For verb tense, I gave him 10 verbs with a visual model for both past and present, and he wrote the correct tense for each verb.

RESEARCH METHODOLOGY AND DATA SOURCES

The sources used to collect data are diverse, measuring both Vinnie's and my own learning. The data sources are both qualitative and quantitative, resulting in a mixed-method study. Before designing the game, I conducted the informal communication assessment to get a more detailed picture of Vinnie's strengths and areas in need of improvement. In addition to the assessment, I spoke with Vinnie's teacher to identify the communicative areas in which Vinnie needed additional instruction. Both helped guide my decisions for creating the intervention. After designing the game, I gathered baseline data using the question cards.

An additional data source is data from the game itself. I kept a running record of Vinnie's progress (i.e., answered correctly and independently, needed prompting, or answered incorrectly) during the intervention. The color-coded cards helped me track Vinnie's progress within each skill area. The fifth data source was post-intervention tests to determine if Vinnie's newly learned skills could be generalized beyond the game. Last, I drew from personal journal entries and a post-intervention interview with my cooperating teacher to collect data. The journal entries provided a self-evaluation of my teaching, as well as an ongoing evaluation of the intervention's effectiveness. This ongoing evaluation not only shaped how I conducted the intervention, but also helped inform me for the creation of future communication programs by documenting aspects of a successful or unsuccessful intervention.

From the teacher interview, I gained some insight into my own teaching and learning as well as Vinnie's progress. I respect my cooperating teacher's opinion about Vinnie's expressive communication development.

She knows Vinnie far better than I and noticed differences I missed. Also, a second pair of eyes (or ears in this case) decreased the chance that I may have noticed a difference in Vinnie's communication because I wanted to see a difference and not because a difference necessarily existed.

Vinnie's responses were coded as correct/independent (I), verbal cue (C), or modeled response (M). When calculating final percentages, every C or M response was counted as incorrect. The differentiation in scoring was for my own knowledge during the trials, so when I presented Vinnie with a question card I was able to determine how much assistance he required previously. Also, I was better able to monitor the amount of prompting given. In determining if an answer was correct, I only looked at the part of the sentence the question card tested. For example, if Vinnie picked a pronoun card and used the correct pronoun but did not con-jugate the verb correctly, I counted the answer as correct because the targeted skill was pronouns. However, I always modeled the correct sen-tence structure to promote Vinnie's understanding.

RESULTS

Baseline Data

Before Vinnie began to play the game, I collected baseline data. I ran-domly picked 10 cards from each skill area and presented them to Vinnie. No prompting was supplied during baseline data collection. That is, I did not model how I wanted the answer to be given, nor did I imply whether he answered correctly or incorrectly. I simply supplied the directive (i.e., "Describe the picture") and waited for Vinnie's response. During baseline data collection, Vinnie scored 40% on tense, 10% on verb conjugation, and 1% on pronouns (Figure 6.1).

Pronouns

Vinnie displayed a 79% increase in pronoun performance between base-line and the post-intervention test (Figure 6.2). Strikingly, Vinnie's pro-nouns performance was the most inconsistent out of the three areas. He scored higher during the middle of the intervention than toward the end and flattened out at 50% for the final three trials. Although Vinnie achieved 100% during one trial, he never again achieved this result, with the closest being 66% (Figure 6.2). In terms of particular pronouns, Vinnie performed best with "he" and struggled throughout the intervention with "they." For example, if the question card had a picture of a singular boy or

Figure 6.1. Difference Between Baseline and Post-Intervention Test Scores

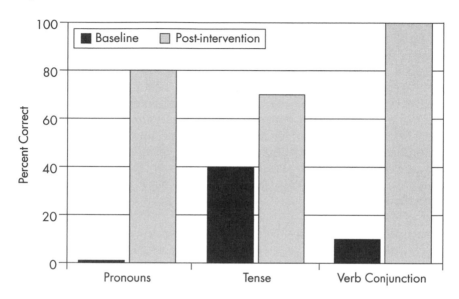

Figure 6.2. Performance on Pronoun Question Cards

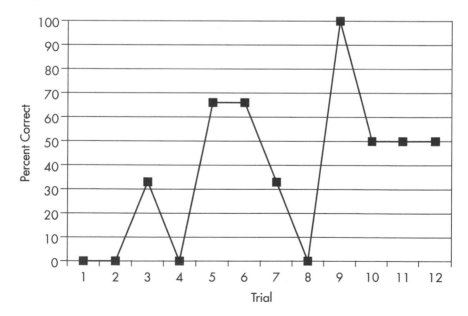

man, Vinnie most often identified the subject as "he." However, when the picture contained more then one person, Vinnie would not use "they," instead choosing to use "he" or "she."

In addition to using the question cards, pronouns were addressed by asking between turns whose turn was next (Figure 6.3). Vinnie had difficulty with this task. Instead of answering "Your turn" or "My turn," he would say "Vinnie's turn" or "Miss Mel's turn." During trial four, Vinnie began combining his answer with the correct answer, stating, "Vinnie's turn . . . my turn" and "Miss Mel's turn . . . your turn." This pattern of responding ended during trial nine and Vinnie began responding correctly and only infrequently reverted back to his old pattern of answering.

Verb Conjugation

Vinnie showed the greatest improvement in verb conjugation, boasting a 90% improvement between baseline and post-intervention testing (Figures 6.1 and 6.4). Although Vinnie showed great gains in this area, he exhibited difficulty with the concept while playing the game. When presented with a verb, he would often restate the verb instead of conjugating it in order to make a sentence. For example, when presented with "throw" paired with a picture of a girl throwing a ball, Vinnie would respond, "She is throw the ball." Apart from the dip during the eighth trial, Vinnie displayed a steady increase in scores throughout the intervention.

Figure 6.3. Pronoun Performance When Asked, "Whose Turn Is Next?"

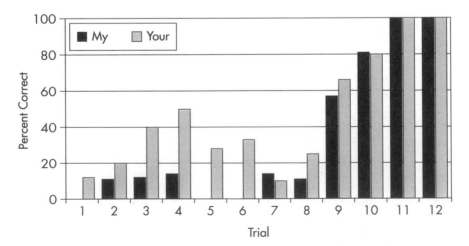

Figure 6.4. Performance on Verb Conjugation Question Cards

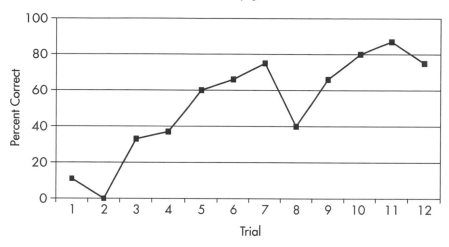

Verb Tense

Vinnie exhibited a 30% improvement in verb tense between baseline and post-intervention testing (Figures 6.1 and 6.5). He had rapid and substantial success with identifying verb tense; however, modifications to the question cards were made during the early trials to help Vinnie achieve this success. At the outset of the intervention, Vinnie was guessing the correct answer. I realized the question cards I designed were too complicated and that if I kept using them, I was just setting him up for failure. Vinnie had zero grasp of the difference between past and present and the meaning behind these concepts and was consequently guessing the correct response. As a result, I wrote "past" and "present" on two cards with an "-s" below present and "-ed" below past. All Vinnie had to do was look at the word on the question card, determine if the word ended in "s" or "ed," and state the correct answer. This helped improve Vinnie's scores.

DISCUSSION

The pronoun results are the most inconsistent and show the least amount of improvement between baseline and post-intervention data. A few reasons help to possibly explain these results. First, the pictures used for the pronoun question cards were pictures of real people. Children with autism ". . . appear to lack an awareness of the existence . . . of others"

Figure 6.5. Performance on Verb Tense Question Cards

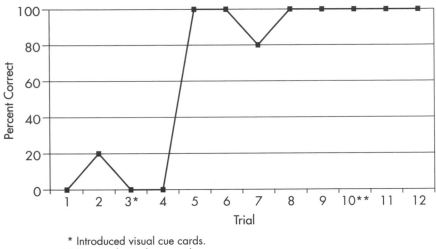

* Introduced visual cue cards.
** Removed visual cue cards.

(Westling & Fox, 2004, p. 11). The use of real people may have hindered Vinnie's ability to gather pertinent information from the card. Vinnie did score consistently well on both "he" and "she," suggesting that analyzing information from a picture of a real person is not the entire problem. Although Vinnie did perform well with "he" and "she," he experienced great difficulty using "they" and often used "he" instead. Consistent wrong answers for "they" cards brought down the total scores, making it appear as if Vinnie was performing at a lower level than he actually was. With no female students in the class, "he" is used much more frequently than any other pronoun; therefore, it makes sense for Vinnie to default to what he most commonly hears and uses in the classroom.

The second part of the pronoun intervention consisted of asking Vinnie whose turn was next while playing the game. Vinnie consistently scored higher when responding "Your turn." Lee, Hobson, and Chiat (1994) found that individuals with autism are significantly less likely to utilize the pronoun "me," choosing instead to use their proper name. Although this inquiry looked at "my" and "your" instead of "me" and "you," these findings may help explain the discrepancy in Vinnie's scores.

The largest performance declines for both parts of the pronoun intervention occurred around trials seven and eight. The seventh trial took place immediately before Vinnie was absent for 2 days due to illness, while the eighth trial occurred on the day Vinnie returned back to school.

The decrease in correct responses could be attributed to not feeling well, not being fully recovered from his illness, and/or an indication of not being able to practice these skills for a longer period of time than usual.

Despite the lower and inconsistent scores, both my cooperating teacher and I believed Vinnie improved most in the area of pronouns, especially in generalizing his newfound knowledge. Vinnie improved his pronoun use during everyday conversation and class lessons. He no longer used his name in place of "I" in a sentence and began to use "he" in reference to his classmates. This further indicates a problem with the game stimuli if Vinnie is able to generalize knowledge while remaining unable to demonstrate the same effect while playing the game.

Unlike pronouns, verb conjugation showed a strong, steady increase in scores. Verb conjugation is also the domain in which Vinnie showed the most improvement between baseline and post-intervention data. These trends demonstrate not only that Vinnie gained knowledge in this area, but also that it is a skill he is continuing to build upon. Interestingly, instead of using pictures of real people, the verb conjugation cards utilized cartoon people. Although the focus of these cards was not the picture but the written verb, Vinnie did have to obtain some information from the picture in order to form a complete sentence. It may have been easier for Vinnie to discern information when looking at the cartoon pictures due to their exaggerated nature. Perhaps if pictures of real people were used, as were used on the pronoun cards, Vinnie would not have been as successful. As displayed with the pronouns, there is a dip in scores during the eighth trial. This too might be attributable to Vinnie's illness and subsequent absence during this time.

Both my cooperating teacher and I found it difficult to test for Vinnie's conjugation skills in everyday classroom activities, as the everyday classroom dialogue does not call for much verb conjugation. Vinnie would spontaneously say a line from the game (i.e., "I am jumping"); however, it is difficult to determine if this was a function of his echolalia or if he was generalizing knowledge from the game. I believe that with continued practice, Vinnie will persist in learning and expanding his knowledge in the area of verb conjugation.

Although the data show only a 30% increase, I believe Vinnie made excellent progress with verb tense. Due to the way it was recorded, the baseline data for tense are deceptive. During baseline data collection, Vinnie had a 50% chance of choosing the correct answer, whereas he had no such choice available in the other language domains. This inflated baseline scores, decreasing the difference between baseline and post-intervention data. Vinnie's progress is more evident when examining the data gathered throughout the intervention. The use of visual cue cards ensured success, evident by the sharp increase just after their introduction; however, scores remained high even after their removal, thus indicating that Vinnie was understanding the concept while playing the game.

The class was studying a timeline of Massachusetts' history, and I used this to reinforce the difference between the past and the present during the 4th week of intervention. One Monday, I showed Vinnie the year 2006 as the present and the other dates on the timeline as the past. I also pointed out some of the verbs written on the timeline ending in –ed to make a connection between the words we used in our game and how they relate to the past. The next week, Vinnie spontaneously pointed to the year 2006 on our timeline and said, "2006. That is the present." That was when I stopped using the visual cue cards, and Vinnie's scores remained steady.

Although Vinnie made significant progress with verb tense during the game, both my cooperating teacher and I believe the knowledge is not being generalized beyond the game. If given a sentence, Vinnie is still not able to identify the sentence as either past or present. This is due in part to the complex nature of sentence structure and grammar that Vinnie has yet to master. Looking at a singular word in a sentence is a much more difficult skill than what was required during the game. Hopefully, Vinnie's beginning knowledge of verb tense will serve as a starting point for him to expand his learning to more complex concepts.

For future research, I would like to more intricately explore why Vinnie showed more success with the pronoun "your" than "my." Is this something that is unique to Vinnie's communicative repertoire, or is it symptomatic of many children with autism similar, to what Lee et al. (1994) found in their study? Furthermore, it would be interesting to study non-autistic children's development of the use of the pronouns "they" and "my" and attempt to apply this knowledge to teaching children with autism. I am also curious to investigate more thoroughly whether the type of pictures used for the question cards determines a child's success with the intervention. Would Vinnie have experienced more success in the area of pronouns if I had used pictures of cartoon characters? Conversely, would Vinnie have experienced less success with verb conjugations if I had used pictures of real people? Last, I would be interested to determine if it would be advantageous to use my intervention with children with other disabilities who present different communication challenges.

There is one main aspect not taken into consideration that I will address in future interventions created to examine similar goals. Children with autism display rigidity in routine and "they tend to want aspects of their environment to be arranged in a certain order" (Westling & Fox, 2004, p. 11). The game board had four squares that directed Vinnie to perform some action (i.e., jump, make a silly face, etc.). Vinnie loved landing on these spots and in the beginning, when he did not have very good die control, could manipulate the die in order to land on these spots every time. As he became better at rolling the die, he would often pass one of these desired spaces and become fixated, saying, "Oh no! What happened to jump?" My general rule was to prompt him to keep playing the game, and we would come back to the space at the end of the game or he could take my turn and perform the action if I landed on the spot. This worked, although Vinnie remained upset for one to two turns after the incident. While his perseveration did not seem to affect his performance on the rest of the game, future students may not be able to let go and it may affect their performance. I have thought about making the squares removable so as to periodically change their position on the board, but this could be unsettling to certain students as well. I think the best action is to have cards students pick when landing on such a space. In that way, the spaces never change, but the action they are asked to perform is always varied.

RECOMMENDATIONS FOR PRACTICE

I believe it to be a benefit to my teaching and my students to assume an inquiry stance in my classroom, as it forces me to think of how to tackle old subjects in new ways, how to educate a range of students, and how to actively reflect upon my own teaching. Teaching students about pronouns, verb conjugation, and verb tense are long-taught lessons. Every student receives instruction on these subjects at some point during their education. With the use of instructional practices such as whole language and phonics, this instruction is fairly uniform across classrooms. Students such as Vinnie do not benefit from this uniform type of instruction due to problems learning the rules of language, the presence of idiosyncratic language, or even the lack of development of verbal language (American Psychiatric Association, 2000; Rutter, 1978; Towbin et al., 2002). Therefore, it becomes my responsibility to develop meaningful and effective techniques to teach these skills. Similarly, I need to examine various ways to teach these skills. My intervention will not work with every student, as it was particularly designed to meet Vinnie's communication needs. I could alter the game to use with another student with similar needs; however, whether I am modifying an intervention or designing a new one, I must address the needs of each individual student. Last, assuming an inquiry stance in my classroom allows me to determine if I am doing all of the above. Am I finding effective, individualized ways to help my students learn? This question becomes even more important because time in a special education classroom is precious. It is not beneficial to either me or my students to waste time with ineffective instruction.

One day, I hope to expand this intervention in order to incorporate more expressive communication factors, including adjectives, adverbs, and semantic relations. Although the game incorporates more complex language components, it could easily be designed in order to teach less difficult components such as affective communication and nouns. I believe that the idea of a game is valuable because it addresses the motivational difficulties inherent to a special education classroom by making learning fun and engaging (Westling & Fox, 2004). Further, using a game as an instructional strategy has the additional bonus of working on social skills. By doing so, I am creating a Responsive Classroom. As an instructional approach, the Responsive Classroom integrates the teaching of both academic and social skills (Winterman & Sapona, 2002). Social curriculum is viewed as every bit important as the academic. By using a game in my classroom, I am ensuring instruction in academic skills and simultaneously including social skills development in the curriculum.

These ideas are not only important for me but for other teachers and schools as well. It is important for teachers and schools to think beyond the scope of current curriculum to incorporate other styles of learning and to measure achievement in varying fashions. No two students perform and demonstrate knowledge identically, and schools and teachers need to support every child's learning development.

At the end of this inquiry, I possess the knowledge and skills necessary to develop a communication intervention specially targeted toward the expressive skills of students with autism. Specifically, I am able to create an effective intervention by assessing a student, choosing an area in need of improvement, developing a plan to address this area, and measuring the student's learning. Honing my intervention skills and developing an effective instructional approach has changed how I will develop future communication interventions.

REFERENCES

American Psychiatric Association. (2000). *Diagnostic and statistical manual of mental disorders* (4th ed.). Washington, DC: Author.
Downing, J. E. (1999). *Teaching communication skills to students with severe disabilities.* Baltimore, MD: Paul H. Brookes.
Erba, H. W. (2000). Early intervention programs for children with autism: Conceptual frameworks for implementation. *American Journal of Orthopsychiatry, 70*(1), 82–94.

Goetz, L., & Sailor, W. (1988). New directions: Communication development in persons with severe disabilities. *Topics in Language Disorders, 8,* 41–54.

Goldstein, H. (2002). Communication intervention for children with autism: A review of treatment efficacy. *Journal of Autism and Developmental Disorders, 32*(5), 373–396.

Koegel, R. L., Camarata, S. M., Valdez-Menchaca, M., & Koegel, R. L. (1998). Setting generalization of question-asking by children with autism. *American Journal on Mental Retardation, 102,* 346–357.

Lee, A., Hobson, R. P., & Chiat, S. (1994). I, you, me and autism: An experimental study. *Journal of Autism and Developmental Disorders, 24*(2), 155–176.

Rutter, M. (1978). Diagnosis and definition. In M. Rutter & E. Schopler (Eds.), *Autism: A reappraisal of concepts and treatment* (pp. 1–25). New York: Plenum Press.

Schnorr, R. F. (1997). From enrollment to membership: "Belonging" in middle and high school classes. *Journal of The Association for Persons with Severe Handicaps, 22,* 1–15.

Smith, T. (2001). Discrete trial training in the treatment of autism. *Focus on Autism and Other Developmental Disabilities, 16*(2), 86–105.

Towbin, K. E., Mauk, J. E., & Batshaw, M. L. (2002). Pervasive developmental disorders. In M. L. Batshaw (Ed.), *Children with disabilities* (pp. 365–387). Baltimore: Paul H. Brookes.

Westling, D. L., & Fox, L. (2004). *Teaching students with severe disabilities* (3rd ed.). Columbus, OH: Pearson.

Winterman, K. G., & Sapona, R. H. (2002). Everyone's included: Supporting young children with autism spectrum disorders in a responsive classroom learning environment. *TEACHING Exceptional Children, 35*(1), 30–35.

7

The Effects of Individual and Small-Group Tutoring on Math Performance

Julie Catalano

The Berkely Elementary School is part of the Mumsford School District, a large urban school district. Berkely Elementary is a pilot school located in Rowland, and it primarily serves students from the local neighborhood. Thus the majority of the students in the school are students of color, and most of the students are from low-income families. Roughly 15 years ago this particular school was among the worst elementary schools in the district, but since that time it has experienced tremendous success in teaching students in all the content areas following the standards set forth by both the state and national professional organizations.

The question that I investigated this semester developed through watching my fourth grade students prepare for a midterm exam. The students were given a review packet, and their goal was to work through the entire packet, and complete each section with 90% accuracy. The sections of the packet included every skill that they had learned thus far, from basic addition to more advanced skills like division and probability. A significant number had forgotten basic operations such as the addition and subtraction of three-digit numbers, the rounding of numbers, and the concept of place value. Many of these skills had been taught and reviewed beginning in the first grade. Thus, it was a concern that by fourth grade these students still lacked mastery in these areas. Therefore, the question that I investigated this semester was: How will the math performance of my struggling students change if I offer them tutoring in both a small group setting as well as individually?

Clearly, this question is directly linked to student learning, as it is tied very closely to their performance in a core content area. My hope was that through the investigation of this question, methods of supporting students at risk for failing math class and missing the most fundamental math concepts would be developed. Furthermore, these intensive sessions would hopefully do more than simply keep these students from failing. By the end of the project, the goal was that these students would be meeting the standards set by the state for their grade level and would feel competent in their own math abilities, as this self-confidence was likely to positively impact further academic work. A final goal of the intervention was to ensure that the learning was done in a fun and supportive environment in order to ensure that the students not only mastered skills, but also came to see mathematics as an enjoyable activity.

When considering this intervention and its implications for all learners in my classroom, a critical look at the math program itself was necessary. Mumsford public schools are required to use TERC (2010), an investigative mathematics program that encourages students to understand the math content behind the math skills that they are acquiring and does not rely on having the students memorize a traditional algorithm in order to solve math problems. In addition to not using traditional algorithms, TERC also encourages critical mathematical thinking in students, and they are often asked to write short paragraphs explaining or justifying their answers in order to deepen their mathematical awareness. Since students are not often taught the most efficient algorithm, however, it may take them longer to solve a particular problem. This may not affect classroom performance, but it could potentially impact how well one does on a standardized test that is timed. Furthermore, many parents have complained about TERC and other "new" math programs, as they have not been able to help their children with their homework. This may not matter in homes where there is access to outside resources such as private tutoring or the Internet, but for students who already come from limited resources, losing the support and help of their parents or guardians can put them at a significant disadvantage. Finally, the TERC curriculum includes a tremendous amount of language both in its explanation of mathematical concepts and skills as well as in the answers it requires of students. Therefore, students with a language based learning disability may be at a disadvantage when this program is used in an inclusive classroom, as their lack of reading and writing skills will be assessed along with their ability to learn the mathematical skills. This may put them at a disadvantage because even if they understand and can solve the basic math problems, they may lack the more sophisticated language skills required by the program to express their mathematical thinking. Thus, I was very interested to explore how TERC was taught in this particular classroom, what positive impact it has had on student learning, what drawbacks the teacher has noticed, and what could be done to supplement the TERC curriculum in order to improve student learning.

In addition to TERC, Berkely is able to offer algebra two times per week to their students. Since algebra is seen as an add-on to a certain degree, my intervention took place during algebra. This led to a dilemma of practice, since many of the lower-achieving students who might benefit the most from an additional math program could potentially lose that program due to their struggles with TERC. Due to algebra being so vital to achievement in middle school and high school, as well as being a key content area for teaching critical mathematic thinking, only allowing the successful students to access algebra may simply perpetuate the learning gap in the classroom. In the long run, this pattern may negatively impact math achievement. Thus, the balance between these two programs and their individual importance to the students needed to be critically looked at while conducting research in this classroom.

The students selected to participate in this research study were the ones currently struggling the most with mathematics. They were identified, with the assistance of my cooperating teacher, after looking at the mathematics data from the midterm assessment. All four of the students selected for the intervention were boys and three of them had Individualized Educational Plans (IEPs). These students were in this classroom because Berkely is an inclusion setting. If they were at another Mumsford public school, at least two of their IEPs would call for a significantly smaller classroom. Although Berkley has small class sizes compared to most Mumsford public schools, these students appeared to still not be getting all of their educational needs met. This problem was further compounded because the paraprofessional in this particular classroom had a tremendous amount of anxiety around the mathematics curriculum and was not able to fully support the struggling students. Thus, as the class moved forward these four students continued to fall behind, as they were without the necessary classroom and school supports that would ensure their progress in math class.

As I began to work with these four students, it was important for me to understand the particular history of each student as well as their educational needs. This helped me to better scaffold my instruction to ensure their learning and helped me to avoid forming any unwarranted bias against them. For example, one student had a language-based learning disability. While he mastered the math content quite easily, he did not do well on assessments because he could not articulate his mathematical thinking. This was vital information, as it would have been easy to believe that he was copying another student's work since he could not justify or explain his answers. Working with him required deep, probing questions to help him uncover his own thinking, as well as worksheets that forced him to show the steps of his problem-solving approach. Another student in the group had a substantial history of neglect. Thus, he had missed key pieces of the mathematics curriculum over the years. Taking the time to learn this information about him allowed me to realize that he simply needed to be retaught the material. It was not a sign of his intelligence that he lacked basic skills such as adding and subtracting; rather, he had not been able to access that curriculum content and needed to have it presented again in order to begin to master it. Clearly, each student had unique reasons for their mathematical struggles and understanding; this allowed me to design my intervention in a way that attempted to meet all of their needs.

I believe this intervention would have been much more difficult to undertake without my background in special education. While my current focus is on elementary education and I am not certified in special education, three of the four students who most needed my tutoring intervention were on IEPs and had substantial learning and emotional disabilities. The intense support that these students needed during the intervention was only possible because I had taught for 5 years in a special education setting. Those 5 years convinced me that given the correct supports and accommodations, any child could learn the content. These students were struggling because they simply needed the content taught to them with more scaffolding and at a slower pace than the classroom could provide. This was an important idea to remember throughout the intervention, especially when they did not understand a concept I was teaching. It was often necessary to go back and review concepts more frequently for them, as well as to teach four different ways for the four different students. Through this intervention I came to be reminded of my own bias around effort and blaming students for not trying hard enough when they fail to grasp a concept, when the reality is that often they simply need the material presented more frequently and in a variety of ways before they can make it their own.

LITERATURE REVIEW

When I began to think about what type of intervention was necessary at my school, I began by thinking about what areas are of the most concern in a typical elementary school. I focused primarily on reading and math skills. According to national data, many students are still not making adequate progress on standardized tests intended to measure students against performance goals. This is especially true for students of color (Good, Aronson, & Inzlicht, 2003), which is the majority of the students in my classroom. After seeing their scores on a math review and determining that my own area of strength was math and not reading, I began to think about what type of intervention would best help them to master grade-level math concepts.

Although the intervention that I am proposing is a tutoring session, my literature review extends beyond tutoring and looks at the different approaches to teaching mathematics and their relevant strengths and weaknesses, since my pedagogical style during the tutoring session would also impact student learning. As I investigated various strategies for teaching mathematics, it appeared that there were essentially two schools of thought around math curriculum. The first approach is an investigative approach (often called "new math" and including the TERC curriculum currently in use at Berkely) and is used primarily in Western nations, including the United States, while the other approach is considered more traditional and teacher-centered, and is often found in Asian countries. While any comparison between them must also take into account the differences in culture, it did provide me with a starting point for my intervention (Zhao, 2005).

Investigative math was just recently introduced in China as their national curriculum. It was adopted a number of years ago in order to foster creativity in China's students, but in 2005 the country was on the verge of abandoning the program. It found that this "new math" curriculum that emphasized inquiry learning might have been lowering expectations for students and causing confusion among students and teachers. It is also possible that it was not as strong as the previous curriculum in encouraging mathematic thinking and reasoning (Zhao, 2005).

Many schools in the United States, also struggling with student performance in investigative math classes, have begun to use textbooks from Asia, especially from Singapore. Americans are hoping to use this rigorous, systematic curriculum to improve test scores and student achievement. This swapping of curriculum across the Pacific is a dramatic example of the "math wars" occurring within the United States, as educators seek to find a balance between a curriculum that allows students to master math facts and achieve on standardized tests while also encouraging students to investigate math concepts and keep a creative mind about all subject areas (Zhao, 2005).

However, another study suggests that these math wars may not be necessary at all if researchers would take the time to see what interventions are truly making the difference for learners in countries with high test scores (Zhao, 2005). For example, Singapore has traditionally had significantly higher test scores than the United States in the field of mathematics. A recent study investigated what might be the root causes of these test scores in order to ascertain if these might be feasible interventions within U.S. schools. Their key findings were that lower-performing students in Singapore are offered alternative math frameworks and goals. While they ultimately will cover the same material as their peers, they do so at a much slower rate and their lessons include significantly more repetition (Zhao, 2005). These results suggest that U.S. schools must find ways to offer students who are struggling in math increased instructional time, additional review sessions, and additional practice sessions in order to help them achieve the goals and frameworks established by the government.

While many have debated abandoning the more investigative math programs for more traditional ones that emphasize more mathematical drills in order to build student mastery, at least one person in the field of mathematics is calling for more advanced work for our nation's struggling math students. This advocate for change is Bob Moses, a 1960s civil rights worker who has become involved in education, namely mathematical literacy. He sees mathematical literacy as a civil rights movement and pushes students to achieve through community organizing (Checkley, 2001; Moses & Cobb, 2001). In each town to which he brings his Algebra Project, his first goal is to get the parents involved and to ensure that they are working to improve the quality of education in the schools. He then helps the community organize and work for higher-level math in earlier grades for all students. Moses also helps to ensure that the curriculum is connected to the students' lives and that enough support is given to the students so that they can succeed (Checkley, 2001; Moses & Cobb, 2001). Given his achievements, I decided that I wanted to integrate as much advanced mathematical thinking into my tutoring sessions as possible. This need to ensure that my tutoring was not simply drills was made especially important because I was pulling my students out of an algebra class in order to help them master more basic skills. Thus, it was vital for a sense of social justice work to ensure that my struggling math students were not denied access to advanced math concepts, such as algebra, simply because they were struggling with more basic math skills such as multiplication and division. Thus, because of Moses' success stories and my own commitment to equity in education, I felt it important to work as much of his higher-level math thinking into my intervention as possible.

As I researched the specific intervention, I found that many are turning to tutoring to improve test scores and help students master basic skills. This is based on understanding that daily review and practice are essential to math mastery (Kohler, Ezell, Hoel, & Strain, 1994). One school system in Atlanta used three different types of tutoring with their most at risk math students. Within just a few weeks their classroom test scores improved. Thus, tutoring appeared to be an effective way to ensure student learning. In addition to an increase in classroom test scores, students in Atlanta also built their confidence in math class and began to participate more. Finally, even though most of the students did not show an overall improvement on the state's standardized test, they did show individual improvement in subareas of the test. Thus, this school system concluded that tutoring was very effective and an easy-to-manage intervention that they were able to continue to expand each year (Bogan, 1997). This helped me to decide that my intervention would be tutoring, since my students cannot afford private tutors and it appeared the most effective way to ensure that these students received the math support they needed.

Finally, a key research study that determined the way my tutoring sessions with the students would be run was an article about math anxiety. It stated that many students have the skills necessary to complete math work but emotional issues, especially anxiety, keep them from being able to realize their true potential (Shields, 2005). There were moments with my students when I could visibly see their anxiety interrupt their thought processes. Thus, I wanted to make sure I ran my sessions in such a way that students felt comfortable taking risks, supported one another, and realized that all their effort would be rewarded even if they didn't always find the right answer. To accomplish this I decided to use a system of extrinsic motivation techniques. This included giving the students math supplies, such as pencils and erasers, for use in the classroom if they were able to put forth their best effort during the hourlong tutoring session. I also attempted to praise all their attempts at problem-solving regardless of their answers. Finally, as a group we celebrated all of their successes, no matter how small, with high fives to make the tutoring group as supportive to the learning process as possible.

METHODOLOGY

The intervention I finally chose consisted of tutoring sessions along with the use of a math resource folder. In the tutoring sessions students reviewed previous work from the fourth grade level, as well as skills from previous grades assumed to be mastered, such as addition and subtraction. Students approached these topics primarily as taught in the TERC curriculum. Thus, the time spent in tutoring was still more independent work, and the role of the teacher was to coach the students as they worked to solve various problems and explain their mathematical thinking. This was vital, as these students tend to overrely on teacher support and I did not want a negative result of this intervention to be an increased level of dependence on the teaching staff.

As the students developed efficient methods for solving various types of problems, they were asked to record this in their math resource folders. Also, as they began to correctly articulate mathematical concepts they or the teacher (for students with the accommodation of having a scribe in their IEPs wrote in their math resource folders) their understanding of a particular mathematical idea. Finally, once students appeared to have mastered a particular type of problem, they were asked to complete a variety of practice problems and clearly show their work. This, too, was to be placed in their math resource folders in order to provide them with examples of how to solve various types of problems they will encounter in math class. Thus, students would leave the intervention time with a support system that they could consult when they needed assistance completing their work in their regular math class.

In addition to the work described above, a few students who were struggling the most had one-on-one time with me. During this time the work was less based on TERC and more focused on building their basic skills. These sessions were short, roughly 20 minutes in length once a week, and were focused on increasing the students recall in completing basic math computation problems such as the times tables or simple one- and two-digit addition problems. This would hopefully help them apply the methods they develop in the small-group setting more effectively and keep them from making simple mistakes on their math tests. If they could master these skills and increase their speed and confidence, they should improve on math tests and be able to focus more on the problem-solving aspect of the problems, while at the same time being less concerned with the basic computation being asked of them.

Data Sources

In order to measure the students' math performance, regular assessments were required. Students were always given a pre- and posttest for every math unit that was taught at the school. This measured the effectiveness of the teacher's pedagogy during the particular unit and not the intervention described above. Yet these tests could be useful if looked at over an extended period of time. For example, if a student typically only goes up by 10 points from pretest to posttest but during the time of the intervention went up by 20 points, this might indicate that the intervention helped the student to learn better during this particular unit. Also, students who did poorly on the posttest might meet for further instruction on that topic during a new unit and after several tutoring sessions could be given the posttest again. Any improvements at that point could be attributed to the intervention, as the unit would no longer be taught in class. Therefore, standardized tests were one data source during this intervention.

Another data source was students' performance on homework as well as classwork. The current classroom system was that students hand in homework on Friday and must redo it over the weekend if it is not at least 80% correct. Many of the struggling students have to do it over on a regular basis or do not complete it at all. Thus, if an increase in homework completion or an improvement in quality, as measured by a decrease in do-overs, was noted, then this might be taken as a sign that the intervention had a positive effect. Student performance in the classroom was much harder to quantify, as their classwork was often not collected or graded, since it was not worksheets but rather mathematical investigations. However, a checklist of both behaviors as well as the quality of the work was created. This was a subjective measure and relied on informal teacher observations as the students worked. If an increase in time on task, enthusiasm, or ability to complete the work correctly or independently was noted, then it could also be a sign that the intervention had a positive effect. Thus, student products, formal test results, and informal observations of their work were important data sources during this intervention.

The data sources described in the preceding paragraphs are all quantitative sources. Yet I was also interested in finding ways to document more qualitative results. For example, my learning was documented primarily in my journal as I recorded how my intervention changed and improved over time. As I thought critically about how I was teaching math concepts and how my pedagogy impacted student understanding and performance, I altered my teaching style. This learning was also evidenced by lesson plans. Clearly, documenting my learning in addition to student progress was important, as the competency of the teacher has a direct impact on student learning.

In a similar fashion, student learning could be documented in qualitative ways. Like my journal and lesson plans, students put together a math portfolio. This binder showcased selected pieces of math work from throughout the year, including the time of the intervention, and any changes in mathematical thinking or methods for solving particular kinds of problems can be seen. This was probably the best way to truly see individual growth and change over time, especially for deeper concepts such as mathematical understanding and critical thinking and problem-solving skills that were harder to measure on a more standardized test. In addition to the portfolio, I kept logs of student activity to see how frequently they used their math folders to assist themselves during math lessons. These field notes helped me to determine if their level of independence in the classroom had grown. Finally, at both the start and end of the intervention, surveys and interviews were conducted to help me to determine the students' self-confidence level and general attitude toward mathematics. Conducting these at both the start and end of the intervention helped me to determine if building their math skills had any impact on their overall enjoyment of the subject area. Thus, this study made use of both quantitative as well as qualitative data.

RESULTS

Overall, both the quantitative and qualitative results from this study showed individual growth for the students in the intervention group. During the course of the intervention the students' test scores consistently went up, their participation in math class improved, and their overall attitude toward mathematics appeared more positive, especially on formal assessment days. Thus, it appears that even a small group setting allowed these students to master basic math skills, as well as increased their confidence, and this positively impacted their performance in the whole-class setting.

The quantitative results were based on classroom test scores as well as completion of weekly homework assignments. For each unit, students are given a posttest that was created by the Mumsford public schools math department. Thus, the format of these tests as well as the academic challenge of the tests did not change over the course of the intervention. Students were selected for the intervention partially based on their test scores, especially their scores on the midyear assessment. These tests are scored on a scale of 0 to 4, and prior to the intervention these students' average test scores ranged from 1.4 to a 2.4 (Table 7.1).

Table 7.1. Assessment Scores

Student	Pre-Intervention Average Test Score	Post-Intervention Average Test Score
D	1.4	3.3
A	2	3
K	1.6	3.3
C	2.4	3

During the course of the intervention, students showed roughly a 1-point increase on these tests. The range of the test scores at the end of the intervention was from a 3 to a 3.3. The individual increases in test scores show that all students improved in their test taking-ability during the course of the intervention. The decrease in the range may indicate that students have reached a plateau. Thus, no further increase in test scores can be expected with this particular intervention. Since a 3 indicates mastery of the standard, these results do demonstrate that students are now successfully completing each new math unit and thus support the conclusion that the intervention was successful in allowing these struggling students to access the current classroom curriculum.

Another quantitative measurement of student progress was homework. These results were not as dramatic as the increase in test scores. Prior to the intervention, these students showed tremendous differences in their homework completion. As displayed in Table 7.2, only two students consistently completed their homework during the intervention.

Despite the fact that only two students showed an increase in homework completion, the two students who did improve did so greatly. One student went from 33% homework completion to 83%. Furthermore, as recorded in teacher observations, this particular student took great pride in turning in his homework each Friday with at least 80% accuracy. Often he would ask clarifying questions about particular problems as well. Thus, for this student homework was a key method for him to receive additional instruction on topics from class that he could not independently complete. The other student, although still only completing two thirds of his assignments, also had observable changes in his behavior and attitude toward homework. He clearly was taking pride in his work and working more diligently to remember to turn in his homework consistently during the period of the intervention. Finally, the one student who did not show

Table 7.2. Homework Completion

Student	Completed Homework Before the Intervention (%)	Completed Homework During the Intervention (%)
D	33	83
A	100	100
K	33	33
C	55	66

any improvement in homework numbers appeared more concerned about his homework and often asked on Friday to have the weekend as an extension. Over the course of the intervention he never followed through on completing the homework for Monday. Yet this may be the result of a chaotic home life and not a true indicator of his motivation or his ability to complete the assignments.

Qualitative research results include the students' work, teacher observations, and students' comments about the intervention during a post-intervention interview. Although not directly measurable, these results, in addition to the improvement in test scores, show the overall gains the students made during the intervention. At the start of the intervention these struggling math students could not complete basic math skills such as addition, subtraction, and multiplication without adult assistance. At the end of the intervention these students were given a mixed review sheet that contained a variety of word problems. All of the students were able to complete 80% or more of the review sheet without adult support. In addition to being able to complete the basic computation skills, the students were successfully able to identify what operation to use in each word problem. These problem-solving skills supported the conclusion that the intervention not only taught the students basic math skills, but did so in a way that they could apply them to real-world situations and more complex situations like word problems.

During the course of the intervention I kept a journal in order to track certain behaviors in the whole class math class. In particular, I wanted to know how often the students used their math packets to help them independently solve problems in math class. I also wanted to determine their level of involvement in math class during the intervention, as I wanted to observe their confidence levels when completing group work. Only one student used his math packet to individually complete math problems in the classroom, but he did so often. This same student became much more vocal over the course of the intervention and in April was observed teaching a new concept to his small group, a behavior that had never been observed before. Two of the students appeared much more staff-dependent during the intervention. They began to consistently seek out staff to scribe for them and to read them the math problems. These are accommodations set in their IEPs. Thus, this reliance on staff was not necessarily a negative development and may indicate that they were starting to understand their learning needs and style, as well as to use their accommodations to improve their academic work in the classroom. Finally, the last student showed no real behavioral changes in the classroom. In fact, for most of March his behavior in the classroom deteriorated, but this may have been due to foster care issues and may not be linked to the intervention itself.

Perhaps the most telling results are the observations of the students themselves as recorded in post-intervention interviews. The students were asked three basic questions: what they learned in the tutoring sessions; what they would change about the sessions; and what they would pick, the tutoring sessions or algebra class, and why. All the students had positive comments about what they learned in the tutoring sessions. These included improving their basic math skills, especially in the areas of multiplication and division as well as finally understanding fractions. Each student now had a more realistic picture of himself as a learner. Each student at the start of the intervention ranked themselves as great in math, but at the end of the intervention this had dropped for most students to very good. When questioned about this change most students said they now knew they needed more help in math, but that was okay because resources such as tutoring are available to them. Finally, all the students agreed that they would opt for this tutoring class in place of algebra because they felt that they actually learned something in this class, where in algebra they were often confused. One student went so far as to say that algebra made math scary, but this intervention made math fun again. Thus, the students appeared to enjoy the intervention and according to their own statements felt that it had a positive impact on their math performance.

DISCUSSION

The results of this study indicate that the intervention was successful. All the students showed an increase in their test scores, an improvement in classroom behavior, and a better attitude toward math class in general. As previously discussed in the literature review section, other schools have used and found tutoring to be an effective intervention for struggling students. This intervention supports those results and offers further evidence of pupil learning due to a tutoring intervention.

The quantitative data, namely the test results, show that all students involved in the study made significant individual gains during the intervention. This is a significant finding, as the intervention was not initially designed to teach them current content area mathematics. Instead the tutoring was meant to help these students to master the standards in which they had not previously demonstrated competency during the midyear exam. This included basic skills such as subtraction and multiplication, yet their test results reflect gains in topics not covered during the tutoring sessions themselves.

The surprising individual gains could be attributed to two factors. First, in mathematics learning new material requires a strong foundation in basic skills. Students who cannot multiply will struggle with more advanced topics such as fractions, since these concepts often depend upon previously taught material. Students' errors on tests were often not due to a misunderstanding of the new content but rather an inability to use basic math skills to solve more advanced problems. For example, the students in my group struggled to find equivalent fractions because they did not know their multiplication tables. Thus, providing them with tutoring in basic skills allowed them to access more advanced concepts and to successfully complete standards-based assessments on new material. Second, most of my students demonstrated a tremendous amount of anxiety around mathematics because they had a significant history of failure with this topic. By allowing them to participate in a more homogenous group where they felt less intimidated and could experience success in math, they were able to boost their own confidence levels with math. Over the course of the intervention it was clear that when presented with a problem, the students believed that they had the skills and strategies necessary to solve it correctly. Therefore, they began to spend more time on their tests, to be more confident in test-taking situations, and to use multiple strategies to solve difficult problems. This combination of an increase in basic mathematical skills, as well as increased confidence in their own abilities, may have contributed to the gains seen in their test scores.

It is also significant to note that these students typically scored in the lowest quarter of the class. These test scores were the reason they were initially chosen for the intervention group. Over the course of the intervention these students not only improved their test scores, but also moved out of the lowest quarter of the class to become more widely dispersed in the classroom data. Thus, the data suggest that the students were much closer to performing at their true ability levels. Even more significantly, during the intervention these students consistently scored 3s on their tests. This indicates that they are meeting, but not exceeding, state standards. This is a tremendous gain, especially since it indicates that these students improved at an individual level so they were no longer "struggling" students in the wider context of Mumsford public schools and the state frameworks and standards. Consequently, this intervention supports the idea that tutoring is an effective way of ensuring that all students are able to master all the material presented to them in the whole class setting.

One major concern of the intervention was that a pullout model for tutoring would negatively impact the students' sense of self. This was especially true at this school, as they follow an inclusion model and students are not familiar with the concept of being removed from the whole class setting in order to receive services. Initially, many of my students did indeed complain when it came time to leave algebra class for tutoring. Over the course of the study this behavior was extinguished, as they began to see the gains they were making due to the tutoring sessions. Other students began to request tutoring, and my students began to ask on Monday about tutoring on Wednesday because they were excited about our sessions together. The data clearly support this observation, since by the end of the study all of my students chose tutoring over algebra class. They claimed that they felt more comfortable learning math in a small-group setting. In algebra class they often felt lost, but in tutoring they understood certain concepts, like fractions, for the first time. One worrisome result was that their own self-assessment of their math ability did indeed decline over the course of the study. Yet when questioned, it appeared that they now simply had a more honest view of themselves as students. It was not a negative in their mind to say that they were good but not great at math. It simply reflected their new understanding that they need more support in math class, and all said they would be willing to continue to access this support if it was offered next year. Clearly, the intervention helped students not only to master math content, but also to better know themselves as learners. This personal insight did not negatively impact them; rather, it ensured that in the future they will continue to seek the support they need to be successful students.

IMPLICATIONS OF FINDINGS

The findings recorded in this study suggest that every student can master grade-level curriculum if given enough time and support. This is often not feasible in a whole-class setting even when instruction is differentiated for a wide variety of learners. Thus, schools must find creative ways to offer all students more instructional time with concepts they are struggling to master. Tutoring is an effective method of doing this in terms of both time and money.

The intervention designed for this study took place over a 6-week period. Tutoring was offered only during algebra class. Thus, it started out being offered for 2 hours a week, and then during the month of March as students prepared for Massachusetts Comprehensive Assessment (MCAS), it was only offered for 1 hour per week. Despite the time constraints with the intervention, students still showed improvements in the areas of standardized tests, participation in math class, and overall attitude toward the subject area. It seems that schools do not need a tremendous amount of instructional time to reap rewards. Furthermore, tutoring done by the school is much more cost-effective for students and their families than relying on private firms such as Sylvan, as mentioned in the literature review portion of this paper. Private tutoring costs Americans roughly $1 billion annually, yet this study was conducted without any cost to the school or students. In this study, the tutor was a student teacher intern. Yet another school district in Atlanta had a successful intervention with community volunteers who were offered only basic training in the math curriculum before becoming tutors. Thus, using community resources and resources already in place at the school can make this a very simple yet effective way to support struggling students.

One limitation of my research is that I am unable to find a clear correlation between my intervention and the results of my study. During the time of my intervention, at least two of my students were also receiving afterschool tutoring in order to prepare them for the mathematics portion of the MCAS exam. Therefore, some of my students received much more tutoring than the 1 or 2 hours per week that I was offering to them. This may have impacted how quickly they mastered certain skills, as well as why they did well on subjects not covered in my tutoring session. Yet, because my intervention was tutoring and the only other variable was additional tutoring, any positive results are clearly due to tutoring. Thus, I can say that tutoring is an effective intervention, but cannot say with absolute certainty that 1 or 2 hours per week are sufficient, since many of my students received much more than that.

REFERENCES

Bogan, E. (1997). Three equations for an equitable math program. *Educational Leadership, 54*(7), 46–47.

Checkley, K. (2001). Algebra and activism: Removing the shackles of low expectations: A conversation with Robert P. Moses. *Educational Leadership, 59*(2), 6–11.

Good, C., Aronson, J., & Inzlicht, M. (2003). Improving adolescents' standardized test performance: An intervention to reduce the effects of stereotype threat. *Journal of Applied Developmental Psychology, 24*(6), 645–662.

Kohler, F., Ezell, H., Hoel, K., & Strain, P. S. (1994). Supplemental peer practice in a first-grade math class: Effects on teacher behavior and five low achievers responding and acquisition of content. *Elementary School Journal, 94*(4), 389–403.

Moses, R. P., & Cobb, C. (2001). Organizing algebra: The need to voice a demand. *Social Policy*, 4–12.

Shields, D. (2005). Teachers have the power to alleviate math anxiety. *Academic Exchange Quarterly*. Retrieved June 9, 2009, from http://findarticles.com/p/articles/mi_hb3325/is_3_9/ai_n29219709/

TERC. (2010). TERC curriculum and materials. Retrieved March 29, 2010, from http://www.terc.edu

Zhao, Y. (2005). Increasing math and science achievement: The best and worst of the east and west. *Phi Delta Kappan, 87*(3), 219–222.

8

Applying Functional Behavioral Analysis and a Positive Behavior Support Plan to Address Self-Injurious Behavior in a Student with Severe Disabilities

James Faletra

Each student in my class has different goals and objectives. They also have a variety of ways to communicate what they like and dislike. As my practicum began and I observed the different forms of communication that my students displayed, I found that some students displayed negative behaviors that were clearly a form of communication. As I observed these behaviors, I felt compelled to teach my students to communicate their feelings in a more appropriate way. I feel this is very important to my students being more accepted into the everyday life of society.

As I recorded in my journal over the first few weeks of my practicum, I found that one particular student's behavior came up quite often. Many times throughout the day Bob slapped himself in the head, and at times this was disruptive to the other students in the class and their ability to learn. More importantly, it affected *Bob's* ability to learn. My research question became, "What happens when a behavior plan is implemented to stop a student's head-slapping?"

Bob is a 16-year-old student who is diagnosed with a seizure disorder, developmental delay, and microcephaly. Bob communicates nonverbally using vocalizations, word approximation, gestures, facial expressions, and body language to communicate his likes and dislikes. He also demonstrates basic social skills using eye contact, facial expressions, clapping, vocalizations, and a small repertoire of spoken words (*hi, uh-oh, woah, no*). His ability to use spoken words at the appropriate time is inconsistent, but he does use pictures, objects, and Mayer Johnson symbols. Bob does not like to have any demands put on him such as schoolwork. Bob will slap his head whenever given a direction or when a teacher stands in front of him and asks him a question. There have been days when lessons are delayed for a short time because of Bob's behavior. On occasion Bob's head-slapping was so intense that a teacher had to spend the entire lesson calming him down and as a result he missed the entire lesson. I also have noted in my journal that there have been times when Bob's head-slapping has taken away lesson time from other students.

Many times when Bob has been given a direction or has to sit for a lesson, he will slap his head. This negative behavior can be perceived as disruptive behavior, which has been described as any behavior that disrupts ongoing processes in the classroom (Kerr & Nelson, 1998). The functions of disruptive behavior typically include gaining positive or negative attention, escape from work, and self-gratification (Zirpoli, 2005).

Answering this question has been very important in my day-to-day life as a teacher and in the overall lives of my students. As a teacher of students with severe special needs, it is important that my students learn appropriate ways of communicating. If they are able to learn appropriate ways of communicating, then their ability to learn will increase. They will be able to interact with others, will be more likely to be accepted in the community, and will possibly be placed in a more inclusive classroom setting.

LITERATURE REVIEW

Current research shows that certain biological, psychological, and medical conditions are associated with problem behavior (Carr & Smith, 1995). Some children may have learned to display problem behavior because it was reinforced by others in the past and because the children lack alternative behaviors (Sigafoos & O'Reilly, 2006). Children can also learn to manifest self-injurious behaviors, which are maintained by positive reinforcement, such as attention from others (Belfiore & Dattilio, 1990).

Some problem behaviors are maintained by negative reinforcement in the form of escape or avoidance (Iwata, Pace, Kalsher, Cowdery, & Cataldo, 1990). Children may have learned that if they display aggression when they are given a task to perform, it will enable them to escape the demand that is being given to them. An individual may also use problem behavior to avoid social interactions. This type of problem behavior is known as *escape-motivated behavior* (Taylor & Carr, 1992).

Self-injurious behavior can also be elicited as an attempt to increase or decrease sensory arousal. It has been theorized that persons who engage in self-injurious behaviors have a need to provide neurological stimulation and that these behaviors assist in meeting this need (Belfiore & Dattilio, 1990).

Since it is important to provide an appropriate communication alternative to the problem behavior, one must determine the function of the behavior. Because it is critical to have a close match between the function of the behavior and the function of the communication alternative, a detailed assessment of the problem behavior should be done in order to select an appropriate communication alternative (Sigafoos & O'Reilly, 2006).

The first factor that should be determined is whether the behavior is interfering with the child's educational performance and social interactions with others. A functional assessment of the behavior will likely lead to the conclusion that environmental variables, and not the child's behavior, should be the focus of an intervention plan. Teachers should first modify the environment before trying to reduce the child's behavior directly.

Another way to determine why a problem behavior is occurring is to ask those most familiar with the child such as parents, teachers, and therapists. These people will more than likely be able to provide accurate answers about the child's behavior. They may also be able to provide ideas as to what antecedents provoke the behavior and what consequences are currently used.

In order to verify questionnaire data, one must observe the child in the natural environment. If the results from the questionnaire show escape or avoidance as the controlling variables, then one might expect high rates of problem behavior when demands are made and low rates when the demands are removed. Observing a child in the natural environment involves keeping a detailed record of the circumstances that surround the behavior, such as time of day, setting, antecedents, and consequences (Sigafoos & O'Reilly, 2006).

When selecting the communication alternative for the individual who displays problem behavior to avoid tasks, it may help to teach the child to request help or occasional short breaks. It is important to determine how the child will request help or occasional short breaks. It may be done vocally, with a gesture, or visually with a picture symbol or photograph.

I felt that from this research I would be able to implement an appropriate behavior plan that would stop or curb a student's head-slapping. As current research suggests, questioning those who have a direct relationship with the student, performing a functional assessment, and observing the student in the natural environment would provide me with the valuable information that I would need to implement a behavior plan and provide an alternative form of communication to stop the head-slapping.

As a teacher I recognize that each of my students has specific needs when it comes to how they learn. I have to carefully address those needs and collaborate with therapists, other teachers, and parents in order to improve their outcomes. This research question addresses pupil learning by successfully implementing a behavior plan that increased a student's ability to learn, and it also addresses the themes of social justice and diversity. By stopping the negative behavior of head-slapping, Bob is more likely to be accepted in an inclusive classroom setting or in his community. Because Bob is in a substantially separate high school program, it is more likely that he will be accepted by the general population of the school and will be able to participate more with the general population if the head-slapping can be decreased.

MY CLASSROOM AND MY EDUCATIONAL EXPERIENCES

I am currently placed in a substantially separate high school program for students with severe special needs. It is run by a collaborative, and my classroom is in a suburban public high school setting. My students are educated primarily in their classroom but also participate in their school and community settings. There are six students in my class, a special education teacher, three teaching assistants (including me), and a variety of therapists who come in throughout the week. This level of support is necessary in order to address the significant physical, cognitive, and behavioral needs of my students.

The philosophy of my classroom is to increase the students' independence in their daily routines and their ability to participate in the community. In order to achieve independence in these areas, students are taught various forms of communication such as sign language, picture exchange, and use of objects and voice-output devices. They are also provided with and taught how to use assistive technology such as wheelchairs, walkers, and communication devices in order to access their educational environment as well as the environment outside of school. They are taught independent living skills such as cooking and personal hygiene, as well as vocational skills and recreation and leisure.

Of the six students in my class, two are minorities and the socioeconomic status of the class ranges from lower class to upper middle class. Cultural and socioeconomic differences among families can impact ways in which they interact with and provide for their children with severe special needs.

When I look at the level of support and care that is needed to educate the students in my classroom, I think back on my education and my first 5 years as a student when I did not receive the support and care that I needed. As far back as I can recall, besides kindergarten, I never enjoyed going to school. Kindergarten was just playtime outside of my home and I would have loved the first 5 years of elementary school if they were anything like kindergarten.

For the first 5 years of elementary school I attended a parochial school in a large urban school district. I can remember being dragged into school kicking and screaming. I had a hard time with academics for the first 5 years of my education, partly because of a learning disability that neither I nor my teachers knew I had. Also, I hated school because of its atmosphere. Throughout the day you would hear teachers screaming at students for talking, not paying attention, and even at times for not keeping up with the rest of the class. Now that I think back, it almost seems as though the teachers were more concerned with discipline than they were with teaching. If you needed help, you could not ask during class because teachers would just assume that you weren't paying attention and that you needed to learn a lesson on listening to directions.

By the fifth grade I absolutely hated school and was having a really hard time academically. Whenever I needed help, I could not ask the teacher because I was afraid of getting in trouble. So many times I would ask whoever I was sitting next to, but of course I would get in trouble for talking during class. After 5 years my parents decided it was time for an educational change for me. I was taken out of my old school and enrolled in Mount Alma, another parochial school. At Mount Alma, the teachers didn't spend half their day screaming at students. They listened and spent time with their students when they had difficulty learning. I began to enjoy school for the first time since kindergarten. I was actually learning. It was not always easy, but I had the resources to help me learn.

When I think back to my days in elementary school, I realize how much teachers can influence a student's perception of school and will to learn. I did not enjoy learning at my first school because I had so much difficulty, but the teachers at Mount Alma began to change my will to learn by simply showing that they cared. I would continue to have my difficulties, but I knew there were teachers I could depend on to give me the guidance I needed.

High school was a great educational experience. I did fairly well but really struggled with math. I always had problems with math, but it was not until my sophomore year that my teacher, who had a learning disability himself, suggested that I be tested. After the assessment, I found that I did have a learning disability, and I began to receive the accommodations I needed to learn.

My experience in the classroom during high school was phenomenal, and I am very grateful for all the help I received, but high school had an even greater influence on my life and decision to become a teacher of students with severe special needs.

When I was a senior my school had a program that allowed students to volunteer full-time during the last semester. The students then had to write an eight-page essay on their experience. I was not sure where I was going to volunteer until someone informed me about the Boston College Campus School. I did not know much about the Campus School other than that it was a school for children with special needs. I decided I would give it a try and volunteered in the preschool classroom. Every day I would do a variety of things such as read to the students, feed them, take them for walks, and assist the teacher with lessons. I absolutely loved going to the Campus School because I felt like I was making a difference in the students' lives. As I wrote my essay on my experience at the Campus School, I discovered that I wanted to teach students with severe special needs.

I have so much love for the students I teach and a strong desire to see them achieve the goals that are set for them. I know that I can help them achieve those goals by becoming a teacher of students with severe special needs. Although many of the students I teach now and will teach later cannot speak, I would like to have the same type of relationship that I had with my teachers at Mount Alma and high school. I would like them to not only see me as their teacher but also as a friend who truly cares about how they learn. One of my main goals as a teacher of students with severe special needs is to help my students be included in their school and community. Too many times severe special needs students are seen as not being able to do many of the things that most children do, but if more people would give these students a chance, they would find that inclusion of these students is beneficial to everyone.

INTERVENTION

Frontloading Techniques and Communication Training

Frontloading is providing as many structures as needed with the aim of decreasing the likelihood of a behavior occurring. These include things such as environmental structures, teaching methods, and materials used.

I began frontloading by giving Bob short breaks within an activity to prevent overstimulation. When I engaged Bob in an activity, I would first give one direction and then assist him in following this direction. I then would allow Bob 10 seconds of rest before giving him another direction. During this time it was important not to give Bob eye contact, physical attention, or verbal attention.

When giving Bob a direction it was important to sit or stand next to Bob because he perceived standing or sitting in front of him while giving directions as too much input. Therefore, sitting next to him while delivering instructions was found to be preferable for Bob. Staff would look at the materials Bob was looking at instead of looking directly at Bob. This was done because Bob may be overstimulated by receiving different kinds of attention from teachers such as eye contact, face-to-face verbal interaction, or any tactile contact. By limiting the amount of attention Bob was given at any given time, this relieved him of the demand level he may have been interpreting.

When possible, directions were given nonverbally. Directions were initiated by simply leading Bob toward the area where he would need to follow the direction. From the assessments there was some evidence to suggest that Bob would likely use context clues and would initiate a task just by being presented with the environment or materials.

Because it was found that one of the key contributing factors to Bob's head-slapping was sensory reasons, it was important to give Bob sensory input before giving demands. Sensory activities such as deep pressure massage to Bob's head and back seemed to help calm Bob before a demand was put on him.

Escape was the other contributing factor to Bob's head slapping. To this end, Bob was given appropriate replacements for this behavior. Part of the behavior plan that I implemented was to teach Bob an appropriate way to communicate a desire to escape or avoid tasks without needing to slap his head. Bob would indicate a need for a break by activating a voice-output device located on his desk that played a recording saying, "Break, please." The following procedure was followed throughout the school day in multiple environments to help Bob communicate more appropriately. (Note: Steps 4 and 5 were later eliminated because communication-device use increased negative behaviors.)

Teaching Procedure:
1. Bob receives a demand and begins to head-slap.
2. Look away from Bob and wait for 5 seconds of calm. (See 4.) Or,
3. Bob begins to head-slap and you physically move his hand. (See 4.)
4. Manually guide him to tap his communication device: "Break, please."
5. Respond, "Oh, Bob, you need a break."
6. Respect this communication and give Bob 1 minute of break time.
7. Repeat procedure as necessary.

If you catch him before he head-slaps (step 3), move to step 4. If he has already head-slapped, wait for 5 seconds of "non–head slap" before moving to step 4.

If Bob's behavior escalated beyond head-slapping, such as environmental destruction, aggression, or banging his head on the wall or floor, Bob was given space or removed from the setting if needed in order to avoid destruction or aggression. After 5 seconds of calm had passed, Bob was prompted to use his communication device.

Data Sources

There were a number of possibilities for the function of Bob's negative behavior, but in order to find the true function of the behavior, I decided to first assess his head-slapping using ABC analysis, the *Motivation Assessment Scale* (MAS) (Durand & Crimmins, 1992), and the *Functional Assessment Interview* (FAI) (O'Neill, Horner, Albin, Sprague, Storey, & Newton, 1997).

The *Functional Assessment Interview* (O'Neill et al., 1997) was used with Bob's parents to assess his head-slapping behavior at home. I sent the FAI home to Bob's parents, explaining to them that with their permission I would like to do a few assessments on Bob concerning his head-slapping. I then requested that they fill out the FAI as part of the assessment/interview process. Because Bob's parents were concerned about his head-slapping, they gladly filled out the FAI. The FAI was used as an interview tool to give me an idea of how Bob's parents viewed his head-slapping, how often it occurred at home, the specific settings, antecedents, and consequence variables that influenced his behavior.

The *Motivation Assessment Scale* (Durand & Crimmins, 1992) is a 16-item rating scale focusing on functions of an individual's behavior. The MAS was used to find if Bob's head-slapping was related to gaining attention, escaping from undesired activities, obtaining tangibles, or sensory stimulation. The MAS was completed by my cooperating teacher, Bob's parents, and me. I felt that by having the MAS completed by two teachers and Bob's parents I would gain valid information about Bob's behavior at school and at home (see Table 8.1 for the results of this assessment).

The Structured ABC Analysis is an anecdotal record that includes an analysis of antecedent and consequent events that occur during the observed environment. This is all done after observing the student and recording the time, setting, antecedent, behavior, and consequence. Because I was in my classroom every day and able to observe Bob continuously, I decided that doing a Structured ABC Analysis would be an extremely useful tool to assess Bob's head-slapping. I observed Bob and recorded data using the ABC analysis over 10 days. Because Bob has a seizure disorder and some medical issues, he was dismissed from school twice during this period, and therefore there were 2 days when I wasn't able to record a full day. I do feel that I was able to accurately observe Bob in all settings that he experiences throughout the week at school on a regular basis.

Over the 10-day period when I recorded data on Bob, I informally discussed Bob's head-slapping with his therapists (occupational, physical, music, and speech). They all conveyed their observation that when a demand is put on Bob he will slap his head throughout the demand. They also mentioned that it can occur if there are no demands put on him.

Through the data I collected from the *Motivational Assessment Scale* (Table 8.1), it appeared that access to tangibles was a primary motivator for Bob's head-slapping. Escape was a close second. From reviewing the data I found that the ratings the teachers and the parents gave each question were in the same general area, with the exception of question number four (Does this behavior ever occur to get an object, activity, food, or game that the client has been told he/she can't have?). The parents both said that this almost never happens, while both the teachers rated it as almost always happening. I believe the drastic difference between the teachers and parents is simply that at home (like all teenagers) Bob does what he enjoys most, and at school Bob is denied things he would like because there is greater focus on his curriculum.

The Structured ABC Analysis was the core of my assessment of Bob. The ABC allowed me to record facts about Bob's head-slapping. From the data I found that many times the antecedent to Bob's behavior was being alone. I also found that the most frequent consequence for Bob's head-slapping was the staff continuing with the activity at hand. From this data it was found that sensory stimulation was the primary reason for head-slapping.

Like the MAS results, escape was a close second. The data showed that many times the antecedent to Bob's head-slapping was when he was

Table 8.1. Results of *Motivation Assessment Scale* (MAS)

Motivator	Mom	Dad	Teacher	Teacher	Mean
Sensory/Self-Stim	8	7	7	9	7.75
Escape	14	13	17	19	15.75
Attention	3	5	5	11	6.00
Tangible	13	16	19	19	16.75

given instruction or a prompt to work, and the consequence was often that the staff walked away. These findings indicate that Bob is trying to escape a demand put on him.

Because four people can have different opinions of when and why the behavior occurs, the MAS gave a good general idea of why the behavior occurs. The Structured ABC Analysis also shows concrete evidence of when and why the negative behavior occurs.

Because Bob's inappropriate behavior of head-slapping interfered considerably with his rate of progress within the classroom, I implemented a behavior plan that would support him to decrease the frequency of his head-slapping. The behavior plan applied frontloading procedures and instruction in functional communication. Frontloading is putting as many structures in place as possible with the aim of decreasing the likelihood of a behavior occurring. These include environmental structures, teaching methods, and materials used for instruction. I documented his progress by integrating the behavioral and communication training data with data on his progress in completing daily tasks in his classroom and school environment.

I selected three activities on which I documented Bob's classroom performance: responding to demands during morning meeting; completing the steps of a school job; and answering curriculum-based, less routine questions during lesson time in the classroom. At the same time I assessed Bob's head-slapping, I documented his performance during these three activities on a simple data chart that I created. For example, I would give Bob five demands during morning meeting and score them as accurate, inaccurate, or needed a prompt. Scoring was done in the same way for when Bob completed five steps of a school job and also for answering four curriculum-based, less routine questions (see Table 8.2).

Table 8.2. Sample of Bob's Response to Demands

Date	Activity	1	2	3	4	5	Acc. (%)	Indep. (%)
3/8/06	Meeting	+	–	P	+	–	60	80
3/8/06	Job	P	P	P	–	+	80	40
3/8/06	?s during lesson	–	P	P	+		60	60

Key:

+ = accurate and independent

– = inaccurate and independent

P = needed a prompt and achieved the correct answer

RESULTS

After collecting the data on Bob's head-slapping and performance during activities, I found that when Bob's learning environment was modified and he received the proper sensory input, his performance in the classroom increased. During these times there was also a reduction in head-slapping (See Figure 8.1).

I found the behavior plan that I implemented to be a great success in terms of reducing the student's head-slapping. Evidence clearly showed a reduction in head-slapping when Bob was given sensory input, appropriate short breaks, limited eye contact, and nonverbal direction. Through my journals and observation of staff working with Bob, I found that if his head-slapping increased, it was a result of not receiving the proper sensory input or the staff member working with him not making the proper environmental changes that were needed for successful learning.

From my research I found that it is important to provide an appropriate communication alternative to the problem behavior. The communication device (a voice-output device) was tried each day for the first 2 weeks of the intervention. Each time a staff member would show Bob

Figure 8.1. Bob's Head-Slappings

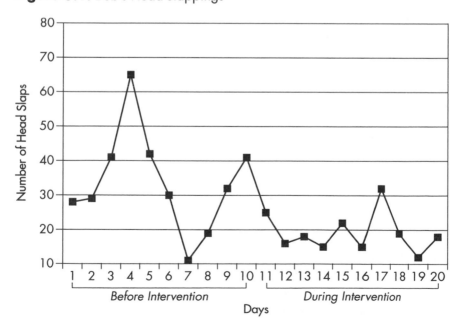

how and when to operate the communication device, his behavior escalated beyond head-slapping. I then decided to try the communication device each day for only a 20-minute period daily over the course of 5 days. The results were the same. The sensory input and environmental changes were providing a reduction in head-slapping; however, the communication device was increasing head-slapping. I decided to remove the communication device from the intervention and have staff give Bob appropriate breaks. If his head-slapping escalated rapidly, Bob was given a 1- to 2-minute break when staff would step away and look in the opposite direction so as to not overstimulate him. After at least a minute of calm a staff member would give Bob sensory input for a minute or two and continue with the task at hand. Some may interpret this as the student still escaping a demand because research has shown that children may learn that if they display aggression when they are given a task to perform, it will enable them to escape the demand that is being given. But Bob is not escaping the task; he is given a short break and then asked to continue.

Because it was found that one of the key contributing factors to Bob's head-slapping was sensory reasons, and research suggested that self-injurious behavior can also be elicited as an attempt to increase or decrease sensory arousal, Bob was given sensory activities such as deep-pressure massage to his head and back, which seemed to help calm him before a demand was put on him.

The approach that I took to teach Bob how to use his communication device required tactile contact (hand-over-hand technique) to activate the device. Because it was found that Bob might be overstimulated by receiving different kinds of attention such as tactile contact and face-to-face interaction, a different approach should have been taken, or the form of communication should involve one that doesn't require tactile contact to teach.

DISCUSSION

As a classroom teacher, the benefit of assuming an inquiry stance such as implementing a behavior plan has enabled me to better understand this particular student and how he learns. I will be able to use many of the principles and strategies that I learned with my other students and in my future classrooms. I feel that from this inquiry question I have found that changing a student's negative behavior will improve the student's ability to communicate with me, which in turn will improve his/her ability to learn. It will also improve my ability to teach more efficiently. Not every aspect of my behavior plan worked, but the process of working on those aspects will improve my teaching in the future by knowing what not to do when implementing a behavior plan.

Through my intervention, I found both positive and negative aspects of implementing a behavior plan and its effects on student learning. From these results I have learned appropriate ways to modify the curriculum for my student through the use of a behavior plan.

The students in my classroom do not have a uniform way of learning. I have learned from my research that each student needs to be assessed individually, and as each behavior plan is implemented, it is subject to change. I want to learn more about how to determine appropriate alternative communication strategies for the behavior plan.

If I am able to implement a behavior plan to stop the behavior by teaching students alternative forms of communication that are appropriate, then in turn their ability to learn will increase. They will be able to interact with their peers and will be more likely to be accepted in the community and possibly be placed in a more inclusive classroom setting.

REFERENCES

Belfiore, P. J., & Dattilio, F. M. (1990). The behavior of self injury: A brief review and analysis. *Behavioral Disorders, 16*(1), 23–31.

Carr, E. G., & Smith, C. E. (1995). Biological setting events for self-injury. *Mental Retardation and Developmental Disabilities Research Reviews, 12*, 94–98.

Durand, V. M., & Crimmins, D. B. (1992). *The Motivation Assessment Scale administration guide.* Topeka, KS: Monaco.

Iwata, B. A., Pace, G. M., Kalsher, M. J., Cowdery, G. E., & Cataldo, M. F. (1990). Experimental analysis and extinction of self-injurious escape behavior. *Journal of Applied Behavior Analysis, 23,* 11–27.

Kerr, M. M., & Nelson, C.M. (1998). *Strategies for managing behavior problems in the classroom.* Upper Saddle River, NJ: Merrill/Prentice Hall.

O'Neill, R., Horner, R., Albin, R., Sprague, J. R., Storey, K., & Newton, J. S. (1997). *Functional assessment and program development for problem behavior: A practical handbook* (2nd ed.). Pacific Grove, CA: Brooks/Cole.

Sigafoos, J., & O'Reilly, M. (2006). Replacing problem behavior. In J. Sigafoos, M. Arthur-Kelly, & N. Butterfield, (Eds.), *Enhancing everyday communication for children with disabilities* (pp. 87–106). Baltimore: Brooks.

Taylor, J. C., & Carr, E. G. (1992). Severe problem behaviors related to social interaction: I, Attention seeking and social avoidance. *Behavior Modification, 16,* 305–335.

Zirpoli, T. J. (2005). *Behavior management applications for teachers.* Upper Saddle River, NJ: Merrill/Prentice Hall.

Afterword: Looking to the Future of Action Research in Special Education

The history of action research and the history of special education are defined by a shared ethos of caring and mutual concern with social justice issues. Published action research studies in special education reflect Francis Bacon's principle that inquiry must be in service of our fellow human beings. Bacon's caring approach to the generation of knowledge is deeply contextualized because it is possible to understand human actions only in context. Action research in special education can be applied to address a multitude of concerns rising from complex and nested individual and institutional contexts. This chapter presents a discussion of a few unique considerations for action research in special education and suggestions for topics that might influence future research. The development of this chapter was guided by reflection about the existing peer-reviewed literature and select topics of importance in the field of special education.

CONSIDERATIONS WHEN CONDUCTING ACTION RESEARCH IN SPECIAL EDUCATION

One of the defining characteristics of action research is its recursive nature, achieved through multiple cycles of action and reflection. A review of the existing action research studies in special education revealed some confusion about the difference between research phases (such as literature review and data analysis) and multiple cycles of action grounded in reflection. In addition to this confusion, some researchers engaged in multiple cycles of action and reflection, but wrote about this process more generally rather than articulating the connections between reflection and action in each cycle. Studies by Argyropoulos and Stamouli (2006); Capobianco, Lincoln, Canuel-Browne, and Trimarchi (2006); and Rose, Fletcher, and Goodwin (1999) serve as examples of multiple-cycle action research with actions directly connected to reflection about participant input and performance. Preservice and inservice teachers may need preparation to identify when multiple-cycle action research is feasible and to disentangle phases of a research study from multiple cycles of action driven by reflection about student and teacher learning.

The process of engaging in action research promotes self-renewal for teachers (Malone & Tulbert, 1996). Classroom action research (also known as teacher research) is defined by its dual emphasis on teacher and student learning, with data sources selected or developed to collect evidence of both types of learning. For example, teacher researcher learning is often recorded or collected in journals, interviews, and focus groups. While it is common to publish multiple articles on a single study, many of the existing peer-reviewed articles do not articulate explicit connections between adult reflection, actions taken, and student learning. Clearly articulated cycles of action and reflection illuminate the connections between what teachers think and do and what and how students learn best. This information is essential to replication efforts and may support teachers to more fully appreciate the extent of their own learning.

Special education is a collaborative endeavor. Collaboration among teachers, families, and non-teaching professionals is necessary to address the complex needs of children with disabilities. The existing published peer-reviewed articles describe studies with extensive collaboration between general educators and special educators, but very few examples of teachers collaborating with non-teaching professionals or parents. This is surprising given the intense instructional involvement of therapists and the investment of therapists and parents in student learning outcomes. In addition to the role parents may play in collaborative action research, adults with disabilities may also serve as collaborators in critical action research studies. Their involvement may be especially helpful to understanding and meeting the needs of transition-age students. Adults with disabilities may also support young adults in their development of self-determination and related self-advocacy skills. With the support of critical friends and other collaborators, both novice and experienced teachers may move from surface level reflections (those that are at a personal level) to the deeper levels of pedagogical and critical reflection (Cooper & Larrivee, 2006) to expand their professional knowledge and skills with great benefit to children with disabilities.

As one might anticipate, there are far more peer-reviewed participatory action research studies conducted with adults who have disabilities than with children. The nature and intensity of participation varies across these studies. It is apparent that "participatory" was defined differently across the existing studies, with the topic of research most often identified by those who do not have disabilities. This raises the question of whether participatory research is feasible for individuals with severe disabilities given the constraints on their full participation. Future research will undoubtedly explore how to move beyond the participation of adults with disabilities to secure the authentic engagement of children and young adults with disabilities in participatory action research studies. It is important to acknowledge that in many cases others, including close family members and friends, may represent the interests of children and adults with severe disabilities, especially those who are prelinguistic communicators. Some may refer to studies that include such interested persons as being a modified form of participatory action research, while others may prefer to categorize such studies as collaborative or critical action research.

ADDITIONAL TOPICS OF IMPORTANCE

The problems that drive the development and framing of classroom action research questions grow out of teacher concerns in the classroom. Thus, while topics for future research may be suggested by the existing literature, ultimately teachers and collaborative educational teams (that include parents) must select a research topic grounded in an authentic issue of concern. The topic of concern should evoke sufficient passion to sustain efforts across multiple cycles of reflection and action. The four themes that structured the discussion of the existing literature in Chapter 2 are used here to organize suggestions for future action research.

Assessment and Instruction in the Content Areas

Assessment was addressed in only a few of the peer-reviewed articles about action research studies in special education. In addition to the assessment of pupil performance in the classroom, action research is well suited to the study of the comprehensive evaluation process that occurs every 3 years for each child identified with a disability. Action research could address the impact of various team models (multidisciplinary, interdisciplinary, transdisciplinary, and collaborative) on the assessment process, the resulting assessment report, and ongoing instruction. Action research studies of various designs could address team dynamics and the goal of integrating assessment processes and reports. Such studies might examine parental involvement or document the emerging and developing institutional structures, culture, and processes that support team professionals to collaborate more effectively during the assessment process.

The reauthorization of the Individuals with Disabilities Education Act (IDEA) in 2004 ushered in a new era for assessment and instruction of children who are at risk for identification of a mild disability. In contrast to the discrepancy model, Response to Intervention (RTI) allows special education services to be provided without or prior to the identification of a disability (Murawski & Hughes, 2009). Case study design within an action research approach (involving multiple cycles of action and reflection) is well suited to studying how each child responds to the levels of support within the RTI model.

Based on the published action research studies about the performance of children with disabilities in the content areas, there is a need for action research studies in science and mathematics, especially the more specialized courses offered at the secondary level. There is also a need for studies that examine how to improve instruction across all content areas for English Language Learners (ELLs) who have been identified with a disability. There is an especially high need for studies that address the needs of ELLs with disabilities who are prelinguistic, including young children with mild disabilities and all children with severe and multiple disabilities.

While the history of special education has been grounded in the identification of relative deficit areas of learning and specially designed instruction to address those deficits, an important shift is under way. Studies by Cheney (1998), Langerock (2000), and Sen and Golbart (2005) reflect the shift from a focus on deficits to instruction grounded in and building on individual learner strengths. The multiple cycles of action and reflection inherent in the action research process may support general and special educators to identify learner strengths. The close connection between reflection and action may challenge educators to examine their perceptions about children with disabilities and to adjust their teaching philosophies and associated pedagogical practices.

Supporting Improved Behavioral and Socialization Outcomes

While non-peer-reviewed documents on action research in the area of behavior are fairly common (as evidenced on college Web sites, in books, and in ERIC documents), few appear in peer-reviewed journals. Functional Behavioral Analysis (FBA) and Positive Behavior Support (PBS) plans are long-standing best practices in special education, with PBS plans actually being a type of action plan. Faletra's study (Chapter 8) examined the application of FBA and PBS to the study of self-abusive behavior in a student with severe disabilities. Action research is ideally suited to measure student response to the environmental changes and the instruction of alternative behaviors (as articulated in the PBS plan), with multiple cycles of action being reflected in the revisions of the PBS plan in response to changes in student behavior. Some children will require both schoolwide and individualized positive behavior supports. The interaction of levels of support may be addressed in future collaborative or critical action research studies.

In addition to studies that specifically address relative needs in the areas of behavior and socialization, action research can support team members to gain a clearer perspective on the emotional or affective side of student learning. Studies by Richter (1997), Capobianco et al. (2006), Spence (Chapter 6), and Catalano (Chapter 7) examined the affective responses of children to instruction. The measurement of student preferences, performance anxiety across the content areas, and affective responses to various types of assessment and instructional approaches may result in improved instruction and learner outcomes.

Inclusion

While there are rich examples of action research studies on inclusion described in peer-reviewed articles, several additional areas for future action research studies are suggested here. There is a need to demonstrate how the individualized curriculum (as depicted in the Individualized Educational Plan based on parental input) and the standards of the general curriculum can be merged (Roach, 2006). In addition, there is a need to demonstrate how to blend the general educators' focus on curriculum-based instructional strategies and the special educators' focus on student-based instructional strategies. Multiple cycles of action within a collaborative action research approach could nurture the blending of curricula and strategies with action plans delineating the roles of collaborators.

While there has been growth in the inclusion of children with mild and moderate disabilities, little has changed for children with severe and multiple disabilities. Gargiulo (2009) reports that only 13.2% of children with severe disabilities are included in the general education classroom, with another 16.9% being placed in resource rooms. For those who are included in the general classroom, there is concern about the quality of the education they receive (Karvonen, Wakeman, Flowers, & Browder, 2009). Mere access to high-level content does not ensure improved learner outcomes, and social inclusion alone will not yield desired improvements in quality of adult life. Engagement with and comprehension of the curricular content is essential to learning in any environment. Accessible physical environments, universal design for learning, community-based instruction, appropriate adaptations and accommodations, person-centered planning approaches, ecological inventory, project-based teaching approaches, positive instructional strategies, and parent involvement are critical to effective inclusion efforts (Gargiulo, 2009; Sailor & Roger, 2005;

Voltz, 1998). The problem-solving orientation of the action research process is highly compatible with the goal of discovering new opportunities for authentic engagement in the curriculum for learners with disabilities.

Amplifying the Voices of Children with Disabilities

Person Centered Planning (PCP) approaches, including Personal Futures Planning (PFP) for transition-age youth, are accepted as best practices in special education, in part because such approaches amplify the voices of individuals with disabilities and the families who represent their interests. However, there has been a call for research evidence of their efficacy (Holburn, 2002; Holburn & Cea, 2007). Collaborative, critical, and participatory action research studies would be highly applicable to the study of how PCP approaches impact student learning outcomes. In addition, such studies could more deeply address how various PCP approaches explicitly create opportunities that amplify student voice. This may include direct instruction of choice-making skills or other skills that relate to the broader construct of self-determination.

Additional Social Justice Topics

Action research for social justice in special education could include studies that examine ways to more authentically assess children, ways to improve instruction, methods to enhance inclusion in various communities, and the empowerment of children with disabilities and their families. Some social justice issues, such as inclusion and disproportionality, are multi-layered in complexity, with barriers inherent in societal structures and attitudes. Some social justice issues, such as disproportionality and segregation, coalesce, making them difficult to define and disentangle from each other. The participation of individuals who have lived experiences in confronting complex social justice issues is essential to defining the problems and to generating potential solutions. Special educators must accept the challenge to recognize and address new forms of discrimination based on teacher and administrative biases and instructional practices that may result in the misidentification of disabilities. Preservice and inservice preparation must strive to develop culturally competent teachers prepared to serve the needs of a diverse student population.

Multiple classroom action research studies can be conducted simultaneously with collaborative, critical, and participatory action research studies to identify the contributing factors and potential solutions to learning barriers in the classroom, and complex societal barriers that limit opportu-

Index

About the Authors

Susan M. Bruce, Ph.D., is an associate professor in the Lynch School of Education at Boston College, with a focus on special education. Susan completed her Ph.D. in special education at Michigan State University in 1999. Since that time, she has published 30 articles and book chapters. Her primary research areas are the development of symbolic communication and the achievement of pivotal social and cognitive milestones that influence linguistic development in learners with severe and multiple disabilities. She is currently working on several research studies, including a participatory action research study with colleagues at Texas Tech University and six young adults who are deafblind. Susan serves as the inquiry coordinator for the general and special education teacher licensure programs at Boston College and is actively engaged with teacher candidates in the conduct of classroom action research.

Gerald J. Pine (deceased), Ed.D., was a professor emeritus, Lynch School of Education, Boston College. Jerry served as dean of the Boston College School of Education, dean of the School of Education and Human Services at Oakland University (Rochester, Michigan), and chair of the education department at the University of New Hampshire. While at the University of New Hampshire he served as director of a Teacher Corps Project, which examined teachers' adaptations of research findings. Following this project, he was the co-director and principal investigator of a study on teacher development, action research, and educational change. He was the author or co-author of ten books and over 150 articles and book chapters dealing with teacher action research, learning centered teaching, educational collaboration, and counseling.

Julie Catalano began her teaching career at Germaine Lawrence, a residential program for adolescent girls. After graduating from the Elementary Education Program at Boston College in 2006, she taught for Boston Public

Schools and created a civics curriculum for women in Mauritius. She currently resides in Washington, D.C., where she works at New Beginnings, a secure facility for adolescent boys.

James Faletra graduated from Boston College's Severe Special Needs Program in 2006. Jim taught children with multiple disabilities in a Boston area collaborative program, followed by 2 years teaching children with deafblindness at the Perkins School for the Blind, Watertown, Massachusetts.

Claudia Morillo, M.Ed., was born and raised in the Dominican Republic, where she obtained a bachelors degree in early childhood education. She moved to Boston in 2004 to pursue a masters degree in moderate special needs at Boston College, which she completed in 2006. For the past three years she has been working as a special education teacher at the Gardner Pilot Academy, Boston Public Schools.

Melissa Spence is a 2006 graduate of the Severe Special Needs Program at Boston College. Prior to attending Boston College, she gained 2 years experience as a behavioral therapist serving children with autism. For the past 3 years, she has taught children with autism at Melvin Elementary, Los Angeles Public Schools.